Prestwick Airport
& Scottish Aviation

Prestwick Airport
& Scottish Aviation

Peter Berry MRAeS

TEMPUS

First published 2005

Tempus Publishing Limited
The Mill, Brimscombe Port,
Stroud, Gloucestershire, GL5 2QG
www.tempus-publishing.com

British Library Cataloguing in Publication Data.
A catalogue record for this book is available from the British Library.

ISBN 0 7524 3484 5

Typesetting and origination by Tempus Publishing Limited
Printed in Great Britain

Contents

Foreword

In the late 1930s, as a very small boy, I went past Prestwick Aerodrome going on my summer holidays and I saw DH Tiger Moth aeroplanes flying. As an early teenager, I cycled a round trip of sixty miles, just to see American machines on the aerodrome. There seemed to be – and there probably were – hundreds of them. Later on, I worked for Scottish Aviation Ltd for over seventeen years and then, after a gap of just two years, I went to the Scottish Airports subsidiary of the British Airports Authority (which became BAA plc), the then owners of Prestwick Airport, where I stayed for eleven years. This minute autobiography shows that I have had a long interest and involvement in the airport and what went on there. Like many other people, I have rejoiced and agonised at the fortunes of the airport.

As you get older, you realise that nothing stays the same, that tides flood and ebb, fortunes rise and fall, and that businesses have periods of prosperity and equally suffer hard times. The expectations of the customers, new technologies and the actions of the competitors and governments are not under the control of any business organisation. Nothing stays the same for long. (After all, some of the great names of the Clyde shipbuilding industry only lasted for a few decades.) So Prestwick Airport is not unique in having a history of highs and lows, but it is still functioning – a not inconsiderable achievement!

This book is a very readable and rounded history of the airport and associated businesses. It will be of importance to those interested in local, aviation and Scottish history. I wish the book every success and I wish Prestwick Airport both success and a long future.

Dr Gordon Watson
Fellow of the Royal Aeronautical Society.

Preface and Acknowlegements

It was not long after I joined the Scottish Airway and Oceanic Controller Teams at Redbrae House at Prestwick Airport in April 1965, that I was amazed to find no record was being made of the events at Prestwick. Scottish Aviation Ltd, the airport, Redbrae and the local area just oozed with aviation history from 1913 to the present day. Tom Harrison, the senior controller at the centre, asked if I would assist in recording the history of Air Traffic Control. This I was pleased to do and I also expanded my brief to include the many other aviation events that had and were taking place at Prestwick.

This year, 2005, promises some notable aviation events: the celebration of the seventieth anniversary of the founding of Scottish Aviation and the Airport, the sixty-fifth anniversary of the first Hudson to land at Prestwick Aerodrome and the founding of transatlantic Air Traffic Control at Prestwick. It is also the fifty-fifth year since the first flight of the single-engine SAL Prestwick Pioneer 2, the fiftieth anniversary of the first flight of the SAL Twin Pioneer and the twenty-fifth anniversary of the GE/Caledonian engine overhaul facility. The Prestwick Branch will again host the Annual RAeS Conference this year, as well as celebrate, on 21 May, the 800th anniversary of the granting of a Royal Charter to the Burgh of Ayr.

Acknowledgements are due to the many organisations and contributors to the writings and the loan of pictures and drawings, including: The Civil Aviation Authority & the National Air Traffic Services, AERAD, the 1911 OS map is by kind permission of Ordnance Survey, H.M.S. Gannet, the USAF, PIK Prestwick Airport, Scottish Aviation Ltd, the Imperial War Museum, the RAF Museum, the Fleet Air Arm Museum, the National Archives, BOAC, AOA, the *Aeroplane*, the Royal Commission on Ancient Historical Monuments in Scotland and BAE SYSTEMS, Farnborough. The welcome support from the Prestwick Airport Aviation and Airfield Research Groups and the many publications of Air-Britain were particularly helpful.

Contributions and pictures were loaned from Dougal McIntyre, David Reid, PAAG, Tom Macfayden, James Ramage, Betty McGowan, I.H. Dobinson, Jack McGowan, David Murray, P.R. Caygill, David Rowan, Vic Currie, Gordon S. Williams, Peter M. Bowers, Ralph P.G. Burnett, James Gemmell, Ronnie Jay, E.C. Cheesman, Quentin Wilson CEng, MRAeS, Gordon Macadie, Alisdair Cochrane, W. Stevenson, Wilf White, Cyril Lofthouse, John Hamlin, Don Hannah, Phil Butler, Peter Clegg, E.J. Riding, Real Photographs, the Prestwick Flight Centre, Alister Firth, Fred Seggie, Jim Cain, Steve Morrison, David Lacey and Brian Pickering of M.A.P. Acknowledgement is also made for the painting *Safe at Last*, by W.G. Wallace, by permission of his son Donald and the fiftieth anniversary painting of the first arrival of a Hudson at Prestwick by Professor Dugald Cameron, OBE, CRAeS. The valuable proof-readers were: David Read, Jim Gemmell, Dougal McIntyre, Dr W.G. Watson FRAeS, Quentin Wilson, Dougald Cameron and Gordon Macadie. Copyright Release takes a major part of an authors' time and every effort has been made to so assign the correct credits to the subject parties. Colleague Adrian Ford ensured that the pictures in the book were to a high standard.

Introduction

Flying activity and the training of pilots to fly and fight is not new to South Ayrshire. In 1913, a military biplane landed in a meadow at Monkton, a village near the town of Prestwick. During the First World War, the Royal Flying Corps occupied Ayr Racecourse and No.1 School of Aerial Fighting was formed there in 1917. A Royal Flying Corps general purpose hangar was erected to house and service the Sopwith Camel aeroplanes. Twenty years later in 1933, the meadow at Monkton would not have become a safe, licensed landing ground for civil and military aeroplanes if there had not been good flying weather all along the South Ayrshire coast. Today Prestwick continues to be the preferred bad-weather diversion airport for many military and civil aircraft.

The story of Prestwick Airport and Scottish Aviation Ltd (SAL) is one of vision, fate, expansion, run-down and renewal. The foresight of the Marquis of Clydesdale and David McIntyre on realising in 1935 the potential of the Monkton site led them to establish The Scottish College of Aviation Ltd, for the training of Auxiliary Air Force pilots, and the later adoption of the name, Scottish Aviation Ltd (SAL).

The action of Scottish Aviation in constructing a Central Scotland Airport at Grangemouth, between the cities of Glasgow and Edinburgh, in 1939 should have resulted in a multi-runway International Airport today, with rail and road links throughout Scotland. This was not to be, as after the war both Glasgow and Edinburgh elected to support their local airports at Renfrew and Turnhouse. The question of the development of a Central Scotland Airport is still raised today.

The aerodrome at Prestwick might not have become the transatlantic air terminal during the war if a Hudson bomber had not found its way to land there in 1940. This led to the moving of Transatlantic Air Control from Gloucester to Prestwick in 1941, resulting in today's Oceanic Control Centre, at Atlantic House, Prestwick, responsible for the management of all civil and military aircraft crossing the eastern half of the North Atlantic.

With the outbreak of war, Scottish Aviation found it could expand its engineering expertise and was soon accepting contracts for the repair of military aircraft. The decision to site the terminal for the delivery of North American-built aircraft at Prestwick allowed Scottish Aviation to further their maintenance skills and they soon became expert at the acceptance, modification and repair of a wide range of military aircraft. They also became the UK design authority for Douglas C-47/Dakota and Consolidated B-24 types of aircraft. Scottish Aviation also had servicing outstations for flying-boats, at Largs and Greenock in the Firth of Clyde. After the war, Scottish Aviation suffered the withdrawal of military contracts and, for a time, manufactured non-aviation articles, but found an outlet, converting C-47/Dakota and Liberator aircraft for military and civil use.

David McIntyre established Scottish Airlines in January 1946, with visions of Prestwick becoming a hub for domestic and transatlantic air routes. After the nationalisation of British airlines and airports in April, Scottish Airlines were contracted by British European Airways (BEA) to fly a few domestic routes, but only until the national airline had sufficient aircraft to serve these routes themselves. Meanwhile, British Overseas Airways Corporation (BOAC) and British South American Airways (BSAA) had established themselves on the transatlantic and transcontinental routes.

The award of the contract to build the Prestwick Pioneer in 1945 led Scottish Aviation into a fifty-year period of aircraft design and manufacture. There followed the production of the Twin Pioneer, Bulldog and Jetstream aircraft, these latter two types after their parent companies had ceased trading, and later the Garrett-powered Jetstream 31/32 and Jetstream 41 commuter transports.

The Cold War years from 1950 to 1990 saw Prestwick as an important Allied transit base, with a large USAF Military Air Transport Service presence, and Scottish Aviation held contracts for the servicing and overhaul of several types of aircraft for the Canadian Armed Forces. The year 2005 will see a seventy-year continuous military presence at Prestwick, with the SAR Sea Kings of HMS Gannet providing air-sea-rescue facilities.

Prestwick Airport was nationalised in April 1946 and had been designated as the second international airport to London/Heathrow. From 1 April 1966, the airport was taken over from the Ministry of Aviation by the British Airports Authority and later operated by BAA plc. Following the 'Open Skies' decision in 1990, the airport, its runway, control tower and terminal facilities should have withered away, but British Aerospace PLC and local commercial interests purchased these assets in April 1992 and after a four-year period of investment and initiative reaped rewards.

The construction of a railway station and 'air-bridge' to the terminal on the busy Ayr to Glasgow railway line and a new M77 motorway from Glasgow to the airport assisted passenger access. An air cargo centre for Boeing 747 and Douglas DC-10/MD-11 freighters attracted scheduled cargo airlines, charter airlines again offered services to the sunnier climates and Ryanair's foresight in seeing an under-utilised airport, available for budget passenger airline operations, with all its cost-saving benefits has vindicated the patience and hard work of the investors and the workforce.

The airport also provides an opportunity for the development of aircraft related support services. In 1980, British Caledonian Airways with General Electric opened their overhaul facility for Jumbo-jet CF-6 engines, which continues today as GE/Caledonian. In more recent times, Polar Air Cargo and Ryanair have each opened hangar maintenance facilities for their fleets of aircraft. The Goodrich Service Centre, adjacent to the airport, services the many components essential to today's air transport fleet. A maintenance, repair and overhaul building has been planned. The present investment programme to re-furbish the passenger terminal check-in area, with supporting shopping and eating areas, together with revised car parking, bus and rail-station improvements will help to strengthen the future of Glasgow/Prestwick Airport.

Peter Berry MRAeS
Ayr
May 2005

Chapter One

1913-1945, The Monkton Landing Ground

The first photograph in this book is of a powered aircraft in a meadow at Monkton. It is a Royal Flying Corps BE.2a, No.273, powered by a 70hp Renault engine and the date is 25 July 1913. The picture was taken during the time of the Territorial Army manoeuvres at the camp at Gailes and along the Ayrshire coast. This was an early occasion, when three BE.2a biplanes from No.2 Squadron, RFC, at Montrose, on the east coast of Scotland, provided air reconnaissance to inform and guide the Commanders of the Red and Blue opposing armies. The meadow at Monkton is now covered by the touchdown zone for Runway 13 at Glasgow/Prestwick Airport. During the First World War, a hangar was erected on Ayr Racecourse to house the aeroplanes of No.1 School of Air Fighting.

Lieutenants Waldron and MacLean, from No.2 Squadron, Royal Flying Corps, Montrose, take a break from their B.E.2a, No.273, in the Monkton Meadow during the 1913 Territorial Army manoeuvres along the Ayrshire coast. This is first recorded powered aircraft to land at the site of Prestwick Airport. (Alisdair Cochrane)

John Cuthill Sword had served in the Royal Flying Corps in the First World War, where he looked after motor transport and general engineering work. After the war, Sword bought four ex-RAF buses and Midland Bus Services operated them in North Lanarkshire. Later he became manager of the Western Division of the Scottish Motor Traction Co (SMT), with 509 buses based in Kilmarnock, and moved to Craigweil House, by the Low Green, Ayr, now occupied by the prestigious

No.1 School of Aerial Fighting was formed on Ayr Racecourse in September 1917, for flying and gunnery training with Sopwith Camels. To house and service the aeroplanes, a General Service shed, with its characteristic composite, curved, bow-strung trussed roof was erected alongside the grandstand. Later the hangar was used as the racecourse tea room, but was demolished in 1991 to make way for a supermarket. (Peter Berry)

Home of the John Sword family for many years, Craigweil overlooks the Low Green in Ayr and is shown here with Mrs Christina Sword in the family 1908 Rolls-Royce 40/50 Silver Ghost, R534. (via Peter Clegg)

Wellington School. Sword had met Edward Hillman, another bus operator, and found he had purchased a 4-seat passenger DH.83 Fox Moth for charter and air taxi work. The SMT management at Edinburgh were also keen on the idea of air taxi and 'joy-riding' activities during the 1932 season and published a list of sixty landing grounds in Scotland. In June 1932, two Fox Moths, G-ABWB and G-ABWF, were delivered to Sword for the SMT at Renfrew for their enterprises.

Meanwhile, Sword had registered his own Midland & Scottish Air Ferries in March 1932, with a base at Moorpark Aerodrome, Renfrew. Sword also joined the Scottish Flying Club at Renfrew as they had the lease for hangars and facilities at the Glasgow aerodrome. He bought the first of a number of DH.83 Fox Moths, G-ACBZ, in February 1933 and there followed a summer of joy-riding from the sands of Ayr and Prestwick beaches and around Scotland, getting the public 'air-minded'. Sword had even grander ideas and ordered a three-engine Airspeed Ferry airliner, G-ACBT, to support his fleet of Fox Moths. Sword recruited pilots, engineers and support staff, including the first woman commercial pilot and licensed engineer in Scotland, Winifred Joyce Drinkwater and on 27 April 1933, Scotland's first female captain flew her first scheduled flight from Glasgow to Campbeltown/The Strath Aerodrome on the Mull of Kintyre, carrying newspapers. Sword's flights were increasing, with joy-riding and charter flights to aerodromes in Scotland, some services in England, Northern and Southern Ireland and the Isle-of-Man. Passenger services quickly followed,

The first of SMT's blue and white D.H.83 Fox Moths, G-ABWB, is shown passing over Clyde House, Seafield, Ayr, in July 1932, on approach to land on Ayr Beach, for some more joy riding. (via Peter Clegg)

Ms Winifred Drinkwater, a commercial pilot with John Sword's Midland & Scottish Air Ferries, flew both joy-riding and commercial flights from Glasgow/Renfrew and the Monkton landing ground in 1933/34. (Alisdair Cochrane)

to Campbeltown, Islay and Northern Ireland. The first of four 8-seat DH.84 Dragon airliners (G-ACCZ) was delivered to Sword in May, two of which could be fitted with a stretcher and equipment to transport patients from the Islands to the Western Infirmary in Glasgow. The first call came on 14 May 1933, when a man was flown from Bridgend Sands, Islay to Glasgow. He recovered.

Later, in July 1933, the Fox Moth (G-ACBZ) from Midland & Scottish Air Ferries departed Renfrew for a day's joy-riding, taking passengers from Prestwick Beach. When the pilot arrived overhead the tide was in, so he searched around for a likely landing ground. He landed in a meadow by the village of Monkton, just north-east of Prestwick Beach, and completed the day's flying there. Returning to Renfrew, the pilot reported his find to Sword, who then asked an early Aerodrome Control Officer from Croydon, Jimmy Jeffs, to come up and survey the area for a possible aerodrome. The selected site was the meadow, to the west of the Ayr to Monkton road, north of St Cuthberts' Golf Course and almost opposite the entrance to the Orangefield Hotel. This hotel had roots going back to 1690 and was to survive until 1966.

The hotel owner, David Sloan, agreed that Sword's pilots could use the meadow and in April 1934 the Monkton Landing Ground was licensed by the Air Ministry and appeared in *The Scottish Flyer* magazine. During the winter of 1933,

DH.84 Dragon airliners of Midland & Scottish were to be seen in the meadow alongside the Orangefield Hotel, both in service and when a diversion from Renfrew Aerodrome was necessary, due to bad weather in the Clyde Valley. Sword had one of his buses converted to a caravan and sent Mr W.J.A. Luscombe to Monkton to provide terminal facilities at the landing ground. Diverted passengers

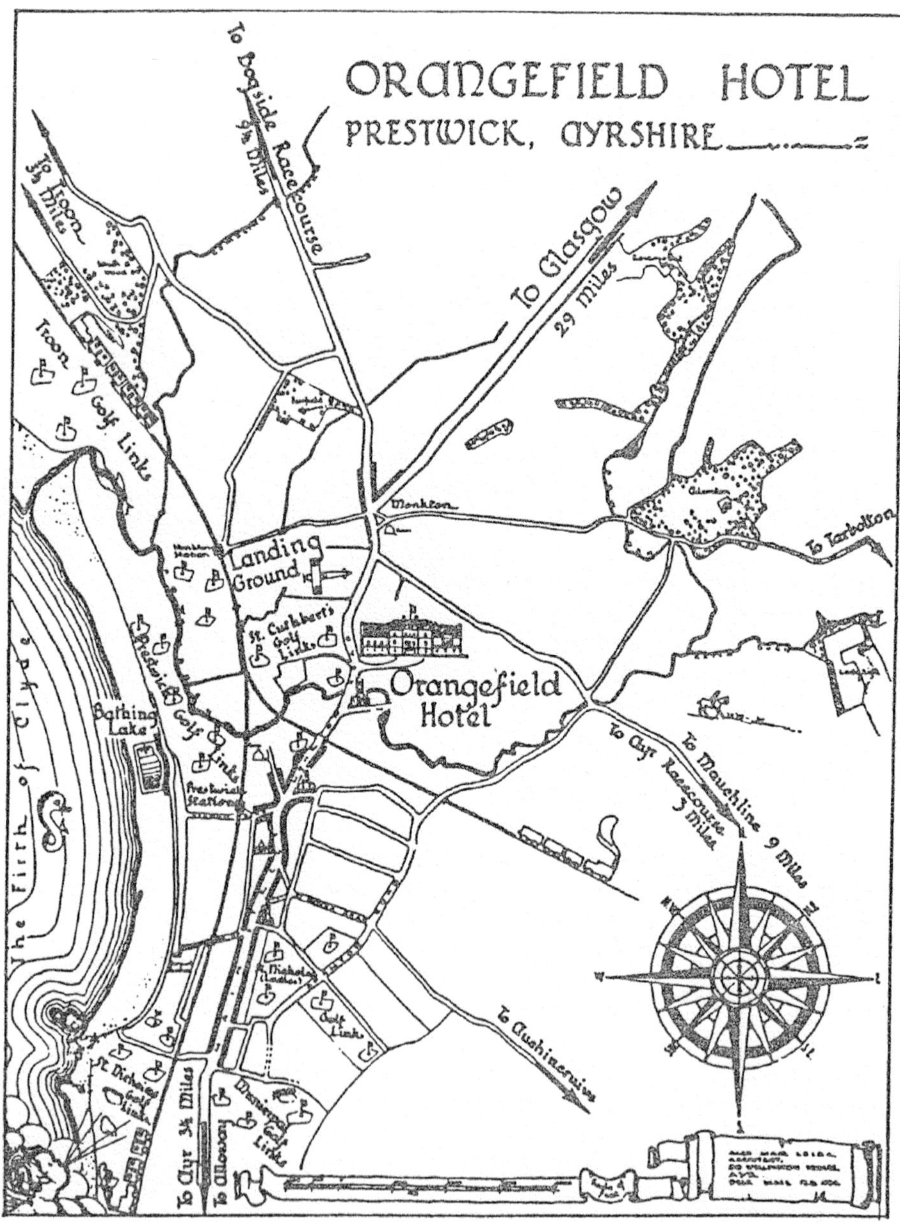

Published in *The Scottish Flyer* for April 1934, the site of the licensed Monkton landing ground is shown, north of the St Cuthbert's Golf Course, almost opposite the Orangefield Hotel. The site is now covered by the high-speed turn-off from Runway 31 at Prestwick. (Peter Clegg)

A Midland & Scottish Air Ferries DH.84 Dragon, G-ACCZ, being serviced at the Monkton landing ground in 1934. (via Peter Clegg)

were returned to Glasgow by car and Luscombe would refuel the aircraft, clean the inside and carry out a pre-flight inspection. Next morning the passengers would arrived by car from Glasgow and the flight would then depart.

In an attempt to control the success of road passenger transport, directors of the LMS and LNER had begun to buy into Scottish bus companies to ensure the continued profitability of the railways. Now, the railway directors of SMT, fearful of the strong competition from Sword's airline, gave him an ultimatum: to continue as general manager of the buses at the Western SMT in Kilmarnock or retire from his post. Sword chose to stay with the buses and by mid-July 1934 all Midland & Scottish Air Ferry services had ceased, except the Campbeltown to Islay service from Renfrew, which continued until September. The air ambulance service also survived. Sword sold his airline to George Nicholson, who continued the routes from Glasgow in December 1934, as Northern & Scottish Airways.

Prestwick Aerodrome

The Commanding Officer of No.602 (City of Glasgow) Auxiliary Air Force Squadron, Douglas Douglas-Hamilton, Marquis of Clydesdale, and his deputy, Fl. Lt David McIntyre, had in 1933 been the first pilots to fly over and survey Mount Everest. The No.602 Squadron pilots were well aware that when cloud or visibility conditions prohibited their landings at their base at Abbotsinch Aerodrome near Glasgow, they only need fly south-west to the Ayrshire coast where it was usually clear and land opposite the Orangefield Hotel at the Monkton landing ground.

With the probable threat from German re-armament, the government had decided in 1934 to increase the strength of the Royal Air Force from forty-one to 128 first-line squadrons. To keep within the Annual Treasury Budget, the Air Ministry offered RAF pilot training contracts to private companies, who would fund the purchase of landing fields, aircraft and provide the training schools.

This timely event led to the formation of the later named Scottish Aviation Ltd (SAL), 'for the specific purpose of introducing the aviation industry in its various forms to Scotland'. The founding directors were Lord George Nigel Douglas-Hamilton, brother to the then Marquis of Clydesdale, W.E. Nixon, a founder member of de Havilland, David F. McIntyre, R.L. Angus, a local industrialist and T.P. Mills, acting chairman of de Havilland.

Clydesdale and McIntyre were able to commend the site to the de Havilland Co. Ltd for the formation of a flying school and on 9 August 1935 the Scottish College of Aviation Ltd was incorporated. David McIntyre wished the company to buy land in the Heathfield area of Prestwick, but the local council objected as this was planned for future housing (still under construction in 1998!). The initial purchase, funded by the Hamilton Trust, was of 297 acres including the Aitkenbrae and Newdykes Farms as well as the 'Cornmill', also known as the Powbank Mill. At first, 157 acres was used as the aerodrome, bounded by the Pow Burn, the Monkton to Sandyford Toll Road and around the Orangefield Hotel, but 140 acres to the north of the road was allowed to remain in crop.

In 1937/38, a further 48 acres of Orangefield Mains farmland was acquired, including the field adjacent to the manor, which extended to the boundary wall of the Ayr to Glasgow road. To provide the site for Scottish Aviation (SAL)

Above left: The Commanding Officer of No.602 (City of Glasgow) Squadron Auxiliary Air Force, the Marquis of Douglas & Clydesdale, is pictured here following his successful first flight over Mount Everest in April 1933. (via Dougal McIntyre)

Above right: Pictured here in 1953, David McIntyre was the driving force behind the beginnings of Scottish Aviation and Prestwick Airport. His visions of the future of the Prestwick site are reflected in today's international airport and the surrounding related engineering facilities. (Dougal McIntyre)

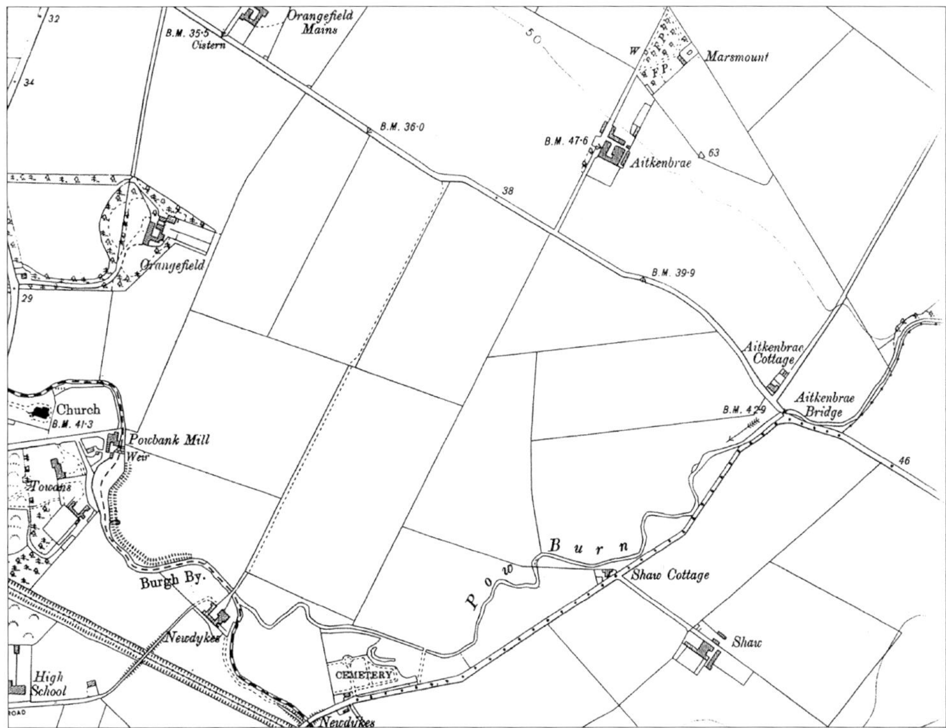

A map of 1911 shows the location of the Orangefield Mains farmhouse, the hotel and the Powbank Mill. The central area became Prestwick Aerodrome in 1935. (Ordnance Survey)

factory buildings in 1938, the 140-acre field was taken over and a further 39 acres of farmland were purchased, including the nineteenth-century Orangefield Mains farmhouse and associated buildings. The final purchase of 10 acres in 1939 included the Church of Scotland Manse and Glebe Lands, bringing the total aerodrome site to 395 acres. The Manse became flats for the SAL employees.

Prestwick Aerodrome Opens

The aerodrome construction began in September 1935 and an Air Ministry contract for the training of Auxiliary Air Force pilots was signed on 14 October 1935. The design of the first aerodrome buildings at Prestwick were based on the second de Havilland School at White Waltham Aerodrome. Completed in January 1936, they included the flying school, administrative building and a 'watch tower', linked to the first Tiger hangar. This hangar, as well as others, was to be used in post-war years as the aero-engine overhaul facility. With thirty-four pupils, eight instructors and a fleet of sixteen civil-marked, DH Tiger Moths, No.12 Elementary & Reserve Flying Training School (E&RFTS) began operations on

16 February 1936, just five days after the company name was changed to Scottish Aviation Ltd (SAL). It was soon shown that a high level of flying training hours could be achieved at the aerodrome, flying every day throughout the year, although even after the fitting of exhaust silencers, flying training was forbidden during church hours on Sunday mornings! To celebrate Empire Air Day, Prestwick enjoyed its first air display on 23 May 1936 and by December 1936 9,000 flying training hours had been completed, three times the Air Ministry estimate.

The Flying School Watch Tower overlooks DH.82 Tiger Moths' G-ADWA, 'DWO and 'DWJ in front of the Tiger Hangar in 1936, while 'DVY and friends circle the aerodrome. (via Dougal McIntyre)

Auxiliary Air Force Instructors parade in front of the new No.12 E&RFTS building at Prestwick early in 1936. Among those shown are F/O N.J. Capper and Fl. Lt D.F. McIntyre. (via Dougal McIntyre)

In June 1937 details of Prestwick Aerodrome appeared in the *Air Pilot*, the school building was enlarged and another watch tower was added. No.12 E&RFTS had begun, in April 1937, training pilots each weekend for the RAF Volunteer Reserve, adding Hawker Hart and Hawker Audax aircraft for advanced training. Instructors from the school found time to formate over the Palace of Engineering at the Empire Exhibition at Glasgow. A total of 50,000 flying hours had been completed by December 1938, proving the kind weather at Prestwick and the drive and enthusiasm of David McIntyre. The fuselages of the fleet of Tiger Moths were painted in a distinctive flame-orange colour, with ivory lettering and silver wings.

Impressed by the training results at Prestwick, the Air Ministry requested the formation of a Navigation School and on 15 August 1938, No.1 Civil Air Navigation School (CANS) began operations with Avro Anson aircraft housed in a new hangar to the west of the administration building. The Orangefield Mains farmhouse was converted to an engineering workshop in November 1938 and continued to be used, until it was demolished in 2003. A new building, known as No.1 Factory, was sited to the east of the farmhouse. This building, later known

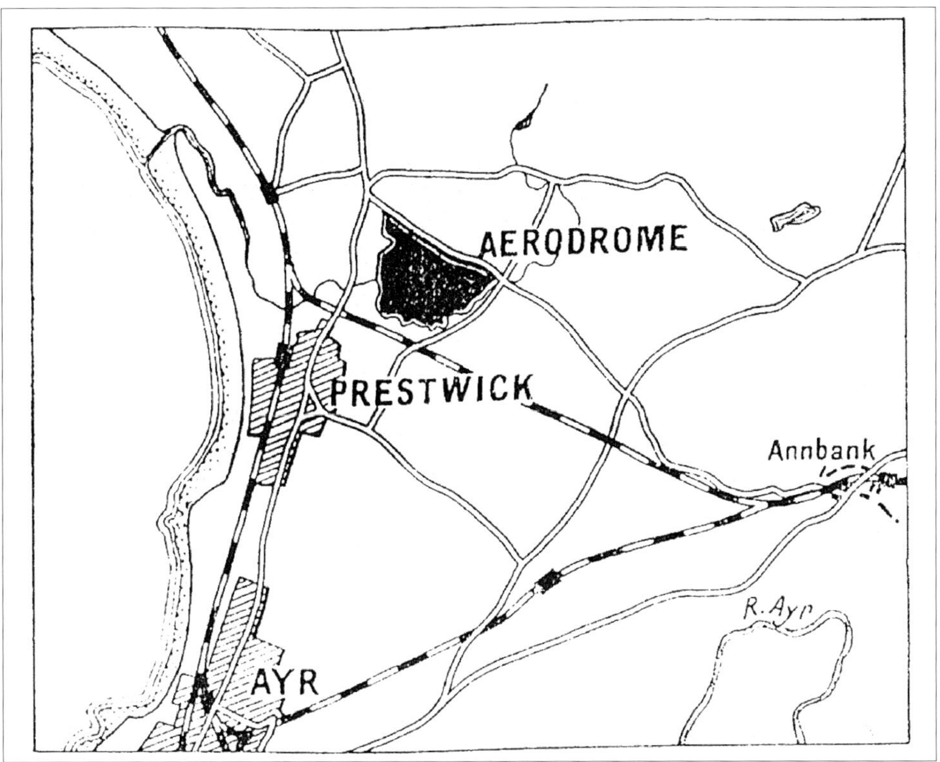

The *Air Pilot* of 1937 placed Prestwick Aerodrome on the map and adjoining pages noted the characteristics of the location. The longest landing run of 1,300 yards was SE/NW. (CAA)

G-AFFA

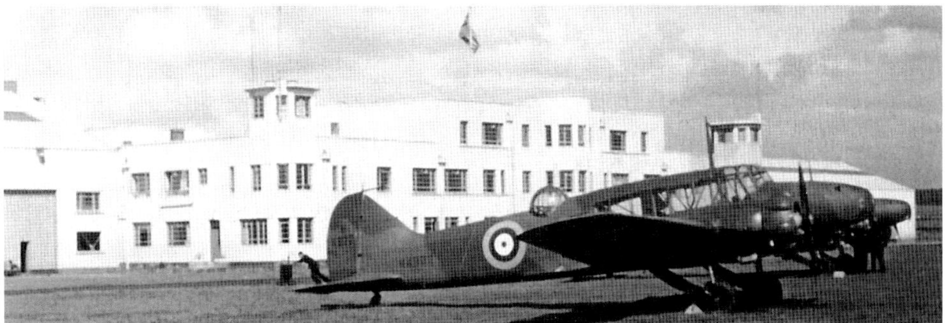

Opposite top: A formation of Hawker Hart and Audax from twelve E&RFTS fly over the Palace of Engineering, during the Empire Exhibition at Glasgow in 1938. The Palace was moved to Prestwick in 1940, as a major aircraft maintenance building. (BAE SYSTEMS)

Opposite middle: Student pilot Alexander McGowan tries out the seat of Tiger Moth G-AFFA. The colour scheme was a flame-orange fuselage, ivory lettering and silver wings. In October 1940 the aircraft was impressed into the RAF as BB813. (Betty McGowan)

Opposite bottom: The Scottish Aviation Flying School buildings, from the aerodrome side, completed in 1938, were based on the design of those at the de Havilland School at White Waltham Aerodrome. (via Dougal McIntyre)

Above top: Prestwick Aerodrome in 1938, with the Scottish Flying Training School buildings across the top of the picture. The hutted buildings in the centre were occupied by the student pilots. Eldo House is on the left of the picture and St Cuthbert's Church and the Towans Hotel are in the foreground. (via Gordon Macadie)

Above: From 1938, Avro Anson N4922 served at Prestwick, with No.1 Civil Air Navigation School. (via Dougal McIntyre)

Several members of this group of Scottish Aviation apprentices, taken in 1939, went on to join the Flying School at Prestwick, including Alexander McGowan, and they later served as pilots in the Royal Air Force. (Betty McGowan)

as the Fokker Hangar, allowed the acceptance of early Air Ministry modification contracts and remains to this day as part of the BAE SYSTEMS site.

The early pupil pilots were accommodated in two large wooden dormitories sited behind the Orangefield Hotel, which served as their mess. These are some of the earliest buildings at Prestwick and still serve as a store. Scottish Aviation had begun an apprentice training scheme and several of the students, including Alexander McGowan, went on to become students as No.12 E&RFTS.

Grangemouth Aerodrome Opens

To provide a civil airport to serve Glasgow and Edinburgh, Scottish Aviation purchased some 521 acres of land at Grangemouth, sited between the two cities, with a central terminal building, flanked by two 450ft long, 50,000 sq.ft hangars. Take-off runs were 4,500ft, with possible extensions to 6,000ft. The Central Scotland Airport at Grangemouth appeared in the *Air Pilot* and was opened on 1 July 1939 by Air Marshall Viscount Trenchard, accompanied by SAL director, George Selkirk. Visiting from Amsterdam was the KLM Douglas DC-3, PH-ASR.

No.35 E&RFTS had already begun training operations from the new airport on 1 May, with Tiger Moth and Hawker Hart biplanes. No.10 Civil Air Navigation School (CANS) was formed shortly afterwards with Avro Anson aircraft. When war was declared some four weeks later, the flying school was closed and No.10 CANS joined No.1 AONS at Prestwick in December. From September 1939, No.602

DH.82 Tiger Moths from No.35 E&RFTS are already parked in July 1939, around the imposing buildings of the Grangemouth Terminal Buildings, at the Central Scottish Airport. (Dougal McIntyre)

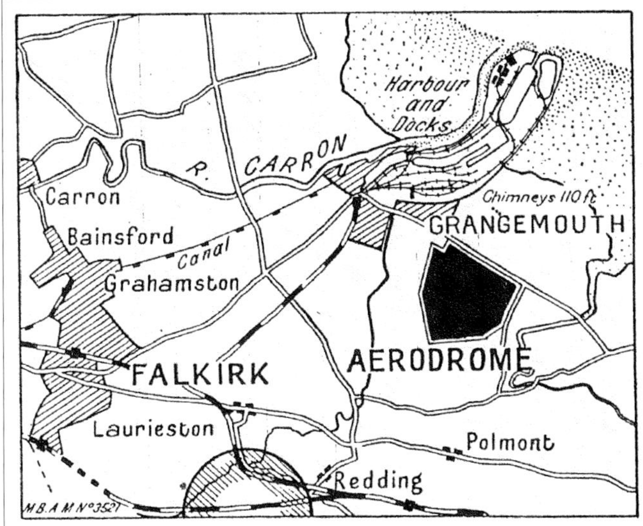

The location of Grangemouth Aerodrome, opened by Scottish Aviation in July 1939 as the Central Scotland Airport, is shown on this 'Air Pilot' chart. (CAA)

Opened on 1 July 1939 by Air Marshall Viscount Trenchard, accompanied by SAL director the earl of Selkirk, the impressive terminal buildings and hangars were soon relegated to their wartime role and the site was not to survive the peacetime hopes of Scottish Aviation. (via Dougal McIntyre)

A few days before war was declared in September 1939, these three Fokker airliners were hurriedly flown to Prestwick and joined No.1 Civil Air Navigation School as 'flying classrooms'. (Imperial Air Museum, CH.17339)

Sqdn Ldr David McIntyre sent student pilot Wally Lashbrooke on his first solo on 9 December 1936 in DH.82 Tiger Moth G-ADWM. In October 1940, this trainer was impressed into the RAF as BB794. (C.A. Nepean Bishop).

Squadron dispersed one flight of Spitfires from Abbotsinch to strengthen the air defences around the Firth of Forth and Clyde. The RAF continued to use the airfield during the Second World War and two hard runways were completed in the summer of 1941. After the war, the airfield was not developed as the Central Airport for Scotland, both Edinburgh and Glasgow electing to improve their local airports at Turnhouse and Renfrew and the airfield was then enveloped by a large oil refinery.

Just before the outbreak of war, in August 1939, three Fokker four-engine airliners from KLM, F.XXII (G-AFXR & G-AFZP) and F.XXXVI (G-AFZR) were flown to Prestwick from Amsterdam and were added to the School. The Flying School continued as No.12 EFTS from 3 September 1939 and No.1 CANS became No.1 Air Observation & Navigation School (AONS) on 1 November, with twenty-four Avro Ansons and two of the Fokker airliners and a complement of 390 pupils. No.2 Supplementary School of Wireless Telegraphy was opened at Adamton, Rosemount and Dankeith Houses, with a complement of 360 pupils. By the end of 1939, the training fleet of aircraft had reached 120. Scottish Aviation also managed No.10 Air Observer School at Dumfries airfield.

Contracts and Arrivals

At the outbreak of war in September 1939 the flying instructors were mobilised and newly promoted, Wing Commander McIntyre became Officer Commanding RAF Prestwick and the Sandyford Road was closed, permitting the joining of the two landing grounds together. With the experience in maintaining the training fleet of Tiger Moth, Hawker Hart and Avro Anson aircraft, Scottish Aviation sought more of this lucrative work. In early 1939, SAL received modification contracts from Rollasons on five Wellesley bombers, also work from Blackburn's on the Skua and Roc. This work was carried at premises in Belvedere Terrace, Ayr and also in a building at the Ayr Shipyard, South Harbour Street. SAL next made rudders for Hawker Hart and Hawker Hurricane, completing 350 the first year. The next project was to sub-contract the building of Lysander aircraft from Westland aircraft, but none appear to have been completed. A further contract came in July 1940, when SAL was instructed to assemble sixteen American-built warplanes that had arrived at Abbotsinch, Glasgow, by sea. This led to the later assembly of numbers of Curtiss Tomahawk, Curtiss Mohawk, Curtiss Kittyhawk, Grumman Martlet and Vought-Sikorsky Kingfisher, many of these at Abbotsinch airfield and Renfrew airfields.

The forecast of new engineering contracts for Prestwick led David McIntyre to search for new buildings. He found the answer in relocating the great 'Palace of Engineering' building, used at the Empire Exhibition, Glasgow, in 1938. This was moved to Prestwick and was completed in September 1940, becoming 'No.3 Factory'. The new factory facilities attracted the attention of the Civilian Repair Organisation (CRO) at Merton College, Oxford, and Prestwick became a primary site for the repair of Spitfire fighters, completing twelve each week.

Scottish Aviation also became the parent company to the LMS Railway Wagon Works at nearby Barassie, where the CRO sited a further repair facility. Towards the end of 1940, the paint shop at Barassie was re-arranged for the repair of damaged Spitfires. Rolls-Royce engines were removed and sent away for servicing and a roadway was laid across the railway tracks to a take-off strip in the adjacent field. Selected staff were sent to Derby for training in aircraft repair and carpenters from the St. Rollox Carriage Works in Glasgow were also drafted in. The first aircraft was completed on 10 October 1941 and was towed across the railway. With only a small amount of fuel, it was flown to Prestwick where flight tests were carried out before its return to the Royal Air Force.

Initially, the paint shop could accommodate twelve airframes and this output was reached in February 1942. To increase working space, two Super Robin hangars were erected adjacent to the airstrip for the final assembly of the airframe and the re-fitting of the engines. They were in use by December 1942, by which time the workforce totalled 240 males and 270 females. The paint shop could now house twenty-five fuselages and twenty-five wings under repair, with ten aircraft in the hangars for final assembly.

By the end of the war, 1,200 Spitfires had been re-furbished in the 'Palace' at Prestwick and the LMS Railway Wagon Works at Barassie.

The Palace of Engineering from the 1938 Empire Exhibition in Glasgow had been moved to Prestwick by September 1940 as an aircraft maintenance facility. It is seen here alongside the Orangefield Mains farmhouse, itself converted to an engineering workshop. (Peter Berry)

Pictured here in 1942, the interior of the Scottish Aviation Palace of Engineering building, No.3 Factory, shows the aircraft present, with Spitfires, Liberators and Fortresses under repair and modification. The Supermarine Spitfire Vb is marked EP562. (via Dougal McIntyre)

Greenock and Largs

To reduce the exposure of aircraft factories to enemy attack in the south of England, Saunders-Roe looked for a site along the Clyde for the maintenance of Catalina and Sunderland flying-boats. Following discussion with Saunders-Roe and the minister of aircraft production, Lord Beaverbrook, Caird's Shipyard in

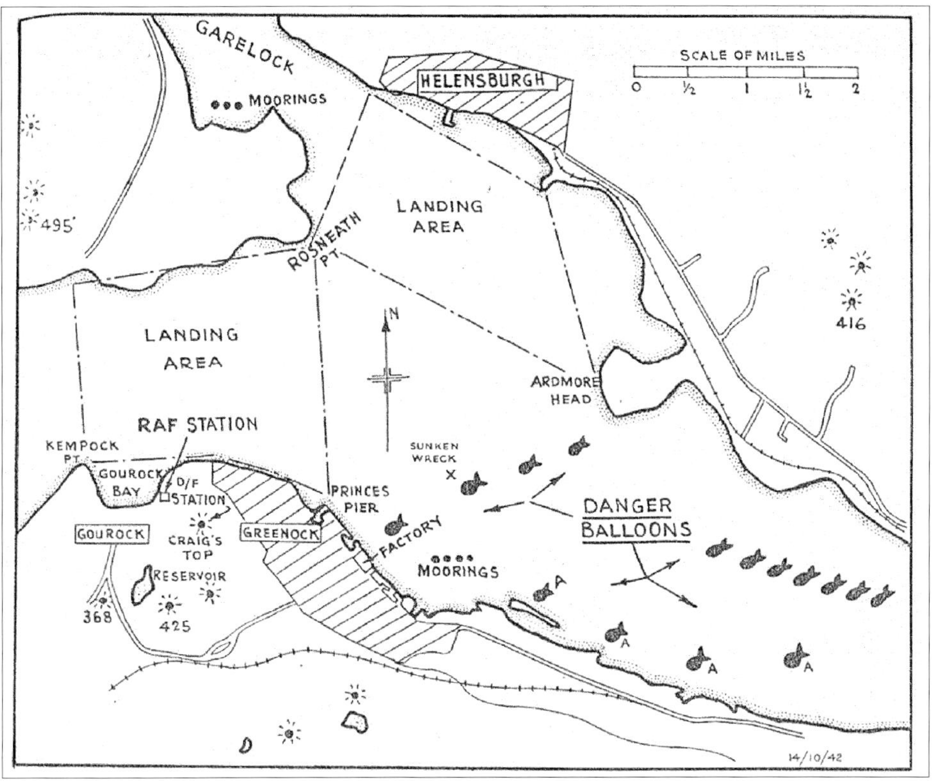

This RAF landing chart for Greenock shows the alighting area where Scottish Aviation had a facility at Caird's Shipyard, for the maintenance of Catalina, Coronado, Mariner and Sunderland flying-boats. (RAF Museum)

Greenock was requisitioned on 1 June 1940 and Scottish Aviation was awarded a contract for the repair, overhaul and installation of radar equipment into these flying-boats.

To strengthen the anti-U-boat patrols in the North Atlantic, an organisation was set up in Bermuda to ferry fifty-one Consolidated PBY Catalina flying-boats to RAF Coastal Command. The first of these Catalinas, AM269, left Bermuda in January 1941 (Fl. Lt J.G. Fleming) and after a hazardous crossing due to bad weather, alighted in Milford Haven, south-west Wales, before continuing to Greenock in the Firth of Clyde. The last of these Catalinas arrived in May 1941, after a flight of 31 hours 15 minutes. On arrival at Caird's Shipyard, Scottish Aviation fitted these Catalinas with radar for anti-submarine patrols over the North Atlantic. The impressed Imperial Airways G-Class flying-boat *Golden Hind*, X8275/G-AFCI, was similarly fitted with radar at Greenock. To complete the delivery of Catalina flying-boats to RAF Coastal Command, an alternative to the long transatlantic route via Bermuda was begun in the summer. Flights were staged through Boucherville on the St Lawrence River in Canada and a new base at Gander Lake, en route to Greenock. The first of these Catalinas (W8428,

Sqdn Ldr Case) arrived on 8 June 1941 and the shorter transatlantic distance allowed future Catalina flights to be loaded with urgent wartime supplies.

To provide additional moorings and servicing space, Scottish Aviation opened a facility at Largs Bay for the servicing of Catalinas. A slipway was completed in September 1942 (and remains today) and the Esplanade in front of the Barrfield's Theatre, (now 'Vikingar') was used as the base. By the summer of 1944, as many as eighteen Catalinas, two Coronados and two Mariners could be seen moored in the bay. During September, sixty Catalinas were in transit through Largs, en route from San Diego, California, to Murmansk, Russia. A further fifteen followed in August and September 1945. By the end of the war, Largs had serviced more than 300 PBY Catalinas for the RAF.

Consolidated PBY-5 Catalina II, AM269, arrived at Greenock from Bermuda and Milford Haven on 30 January 1941. Flown by Fl. Lt J.G. Fleming, RAF, the hazardous crossing took 28 hours 50 minutes and due to a jammed autopilot both ailerons were lost en route. It is shown as 'K' of No.240 Squadron, RAF. (IWM. CH.18057)

One of three large Short flying-boats for the Imperial Airways transatlantic route, G-AFCI *Golden Hind* was impressed into the RAF in July 1940 as X8475. It was flown to Caird's Shipyard in Greenock, where Scottish Aviation installed radar equipment for anti-submarine operations over the North Atlantic. (via Dougal McIntyre)

From August 1943, twenty-seven twin-engine Martin Mariner flying-boats were delivered to Largs. Six of these were flown by No.524 Squadron, RAF, from Oban, but they were not a success and were returned to the United States in 1944. During the summers of 1944 and 1945, regular four-engine Consolidated PB2Y-3B Coronado flying-boat services, carrying passengers and mail, were flown by No.231 Squadron, RAF, from Montreal/Boucherville, via Gander Lake, terminating their transatlantic crossings at Largs. Westbound services were routed via Iceland, for a re-fuelling stop. Twenty-three return flights were made in 1944 and from May 1945 two return flights were made each week to the end of September, for a total of 169 crossings. In March 1946, at least four of the Coronados were scuttled off the island of Little Cumbrae.

Delivered to Largs on 14 October 1943, Martin PBM-3B Mariner GR.I, JX107 was later joined by twenty-six others, six of which were flown from Oban by No.524 Squadron RAF. The type was not adopted and they were returned to the United States. (IWM CH.2769)

Delivered from Gander Lake to Largs on 16 September 1943, Consolidated PB2Y-3B Coronado GR.I, JX495, was joined by nine others. From June 1944 to January1946 No.231 Squadron, RAF, flew passengers and mail services from Boucherville/Montreal to Largs in these Coronados, returning to Canada via Iceland. (Imperial War Museum, CH.2768)

Aircraft maintenance work had been inspected by the Ministry of Aircraft Production, until March 1942, when the MAP approved the Design Organisation of Scottish Aviation to inspect their own work. In December that year, David McIntyre visited Consolidated Aircraft in California, manufacturers of the Catalina and Liberator. Here, he gained approval for Scottish Aviation to modify their products to bring them up to British operational standards.

Air Defence

To provide fighter defence against air raids on industrial targets in Glasgow, a number of RAF Squadrons from Fighter Command were based at Prestwick during 1940, later moving to nearby Ayr/Heathfield. These included No.602 (City of Glasgow) and No.603 (City of Edinburgh) Spitfire Squadrons of Fighter Command, and later, No.610 Spitfire, No.141 Defiant, No.253, No.615 and No.1 RCAF Hurricane Squadrons. These squadrons were controlled by the Fighter Command Operations Room, sited in the attic of the Powbank Mill,

The Powbank Mill was used as the Approach Control Centre from October 1940, the Fighter Command Operations Room from January 1941 and the Transatlantic Air Control Centre (TAC) the following August. After the move of TAC to Redbrae in November, the mill was used as the setting for No.602 (City of Glasgow) Squadron, during the filming of *A Yank in the RAF*. (via Tom Macfayden)

under the Turnhouse Sector. On 13 March 1941, during the first large-scale enemy attack on Glasgow, P/O Denby of No.600 (City of London) Squadron from RAF Drem, flying a Bristol Blenheim, destroyed a Heinkel 111 over Prestwick, which crashed above Drumshang by Dunure. The four crew members were captured, after setting fire to their bomber. During six weeks in September and October 1940, Bomber Command loaned No.102 Squadron of Whitleys to Coastal Command for convoy escort duties, operating out of Prestwick. On 4 April 1941, the Fighter Operations Room was re-located in Rosemount House on the Ayr to Kilmarnock Road.

In September 1940, No.4 Ferry Pool of the Air Transport Auxiliary (ATA) moved into their headquarters, a derelict single-deck bus body parked on the north side of the aerodrome. The task of Captain A.S. White and these civilian men and women pilots was to ferry arriving aircraft, modified by Scottish Aviation, to RAF Maintenance Units throughout the UK. Later, the ATA headquarters was housed in a building complex alongside the Tarbolton Road. An Aircraft Interception/Air-Surface Vessel (AI/ASV Radar) School was formed at Prestwick in October 1940, with six Bristol Blenheim aircraft. This unit was re-designated No.3 Radio School from 27 December 1940.

At nearby Ayr/Heathfield, the site was acquired by the Air Ministry for a three-runway airfield for RAF Fighter Command. Begun in October 1940, work was not going well, when the new CO, Wing Commander T.L.E.B. Guinness MP, a Royal Auxiliary Air Force officer, arrived. The workforce had not been paid by the Air Ministry and it is alleged that Guinness gave them his personal cheque to get construction started again. The airfield became operational on 7 April 1941.

The newly fledged Air Transport Auxiliary pilots of No.4 Ferry Pilot Pool arrived at Prestwick in September 1940 to find no accommodation was available for them. A derelict bus was used as their first headquarters, the Officer Commanding, Captain A.S. White, using the driver's cab as his office. (E.C. Cheesman)

The pre-war Scottish Aviation 'Watch Office' on the north side of Prestwick Aerodrome was initially used by the RAF duty pilot. To assist the air-training of the navigators, in October 1940, an Approach Control facility was established in the Powbank Mill at Prestwick, with communications radio, an HF direction finding station and a Radio Track Guide.

A detachment of the RAF Regiment safeguarded the airfield, together with anti-aircraft defences, and the Royal Observer Corps had their headquarters in Ayr High Street.

Transatlantic Deliveries

The next event in the history of Prestwick was to have a far-reaching effect. Conscious of the threat of the German U-boat to sea-borne food, oil, aircraft and war supplies across the North Atlantic Ocean, Prime Minister Churchill gave high priority to the formation of fifteen air squadrons for RAF Coastal Command. To equip these squadrons, Lord Beaverbrook, Minister of Aircraft Production, proposed to deliver by air the urgently needed Lockheed Hudson patrol aircraft. The urgency of the situation may be judged from the 'Instruction to Proceed'. Senior British Overseas Airways Corporation (BOAC) transatlantic Captain D.C.T. Bennett was called before the Minister: 'Can you air ferry planes from Canada to Britain?' asked Beaverbrook. 'Yes' replied Bennett. 'Right, off you go', instructed the minister.

The risk involved in air-ferrying military aircraft across the North Atlantic was considered acceptable, as this would reduce the transit time from four months to ten days, save shipping space and avoid the serious losses to U-boats. In the event, only a small number of losses were experienced with the British Transatlantic Air Ferry during the five long years of war.

Sir Edward Beatty of Canadian Pacific Railways and Mr G.E. Woods Humphery, former managing director of Imperial Airways, were tasked with the dispatch of aircraft from North America. The resulting Atlantic Ferry Organisation (ATFERO), under the direction of Mr J.P. Bickell, was up and running by July 1940.

With ATFERO headquarters at St Hubert in Montreal and the completion of land-based airport facilities at Gander in October, it was now possible to dispatch aircraft across the North Atlantic to the nearest airfield in the UK, Aldergrove, Northern Ireland. To ensure the safe navigation of these aircraft across the North Atlantic, it was decided to fly a group of aircraft in formation, with an experienced BOAC navigating pilot in command. The first Hudson arrived at Gander on 28 October 1940 and the first group of seven Hudsons, led by Captain Bennett, departed Gander on 9 November, arriving safely at Aldergrove the following day after a flight of eleven hours.

Diversions to Prestwick

The formation flight of Hudsons to Aldergrove was repeated on 28/29 November, led by Captain R.H. Page and again on 17/18 December, led by Captain A.G. Store. Due to poor weather conditions, one Hudson from each of these formations became separated and, using the radio direction-finding station at Prestwick, arrived above the aerodrome, circled and after a few moments landed. Aircraft engineer Matt Dryden was sent out on his bicycle to see what this aircraft was. He remembers the 'rather scruffy-looking' crew in civilian clothes and took them to the Watch Office to 'Book In'. 'What is it and where are you from?' enquired the duty pilot. 'One Hudson, T9426, on delivery to the RAF', replied the captain, 'We left Gander just over ten hours ago'. The duty pilot entered the details in his log, with the names of the crew: Captain 'Pat' Eves, First Officer Donald Anderson and Radio Officer Godfrey. There was a silence and then it was realised that this crew had just flown their new Hudson bomber across the North Atlantic! It later transpired that Eves had left some golf clubs at Prestwick and Anderson had his wife living in Crieff! This scenario was repeated, with the next formation of Hudsons from Gander, when Captain R. Stafford arrived at Prestwick, with Hudson, T9440, on 17 December.

The last formation of four Hudsons to Aldergrove was led by Captain Bennett, arriving there on 29 December. Thereafter single flights were made, due to the difficulties of the time taken to assemble a formation and, once airborne, the stress of flying in formation in cloud, at night and in poor weather conditions. There was also the problem of the slow-return sea passage for ferry crews.

Captain Bennett also changed the destination of the ferry flights to Prestwick due to its fine weather record and proximity to the Great Circle, North Atlantic air routes. The first of these direct Gander-Prestwick Hudson flights, flown by Captain R. Allen in T9464, landed on 11 February 1941.

Lockheed Hudson III, T9426, for RAF Coastal Command, unexpectedly landed at Prestwick on 29 November 1940, 'Safe at Last'. Captain Pat Eves had found a fine weather diversion after the long flight from Canada. (From a painting by W.G. Wallace)

David McIntyre later celebrated the first transatlantic Hudson arrival with an annual dinner in the Orangefield Terminal. Following his death in 1957, the dinner continues to be commemorated as the McIntyre Memorial Dinner and Lecture, held each year, at the January meeting of the Prestwick Branch of the Royal Aeronautical Society.

Transatlantic Terminal and Control

Following a disastrous fire on 3 February 1941, which gutted the pre-war flying training administration offices and Watch Office at Prestwick and took the lives of seven people, Scottish Aviation Ltd took over a wing in the Orangefield Hotel, for the company offices. A temporary flying control tower was then built on top of the pitched roof of the hotel. The hotel and its annexe were then requisitioned for war service by Scottish Aviation Ltd on behalf of the Ministry of Aircraft Production. To accept the increasing number of aircraft expected to arrive at Prestwick from North America, a Civilian Reception Party was formed by Scottish Aviation in November 1940 to cater for the welcome, feeding and accommodation of both crew and passengers in the Orangefield Hotel.

With Sqdn Ldr Jimmy Jeffs, RAF, in charge, it became the major terminal building in Great Britain for transatlantic landplane arrivals and departures. To smooth the hand-over of American-built aircraft to the British, RAF Ferry Command took over control of ATFERO on 20 July 1941, with Air Chief Marshall Sir Frederick Bowhill in command.

On 2 July 1941, Prestwick was requisitioned for war purposes and was transferred from Scottish Aviation Ltd to the Air Ministry. RAF Station Prestwick came under Technical Training Command, which was also responsible for the operation of No.1 AONS, No.12 EFTS and No.3 Radio School with its

An early USAAF arrival at Prestwick, Douglas C-47 Skytrain, AF41-7817, is shown on 7 July 1942, in front of the Orangefield Terminal with its early control tower. (Imperial War Museum, CH.18057)

Blackburn Botha aircraft. To avoid the wartime skies, on 19 July 1941 all initial flying training ceased at Prestwick and moved to North America and South Africa, under the Empire Air Training Scheme. Scottish Aviation and the Units at Prestwick had trained a total of 1,344 pilots for a total of 88,477 flying hours, and 1,994 air observers and 1,200 wireless operators for a total of 134,530 hours. Their training fleet had grown to forty-five Tiger Moths and forty-two Avro Anson aircraft.

An RAF Transatlantic Reception and Dispatch Unit (TRDU) then took over the duties of the SAL Civilian Reception Party. The reception desk was in the Orangefield Terminal and overnight accommodation for up to 139 persons could be arranged in the nearby Towans and Auchencoyle hotels, as well as in the thirty bedrooms in the annexe building. During the war, more than 500,000 people signed the sixteen visitor books in the terminal.

Prestwick was still a grass aerodrome, but with the increasing number of Lockheed Hudson, Boeing Fortress and Consolidated Liberator aircraft expected to arrive, occasionally the newly completed three hard runways had to be made use of, at nearby Ayr/Heathfield airfield. With the Hudson flights becoming routine across the Atlantic, the first of twenty Boeing B-17C Flying Fortress Mk.I bombers (AN518-537) arrived at Gander in March 1941, before their transatlantic crossing. The first Fortress (AN534) left Gander on 13 April, arriving at Ayr/Heathfield after a flight of 8 hours 49 minutes. Additional aircraft were flown across during the next two months, arriving at Prestwick or Ayr/Heathfield, and including one landing at Squire's Gate (Blackpool) and one at Leuchars on the east coast of Scotland. The last of the twenty Fortresses (AN518) landed at Prestwick on 14 June.

The Transatlantic Air Control (TAC) Centre was formed on 15 August 1941 and joined the Approach Control Unit in the Powbank Mill, providing a local control service until permanent quarters were completed at nearby Redbrae

Fl. Lt Clark, RNZAF, delivered this RAF Boeing B-17C Fortress I, AN529, to Prestwick on 16 April 1941, after a flight from Gander in 10 hours 6 minutes. It was flown on operations by No.90 Squadron, RAF. (Imperial War Museum, F.(MOS) 275)

Taken by No.1 Camouflage Unit, RAF, on 18 May 1941, an aerial picture of Ayr/Heathfield, shows the runways, control tower and hangars. Alongside the hangars are two of the early RAF Boeing B-17C Fortress Mk.I, which had arrived during the month. (RCAHMS CAM No.949)

House. TAC moved into Redbrae on 6 November 1941 and at 3 p.m. on that day assumed Master Control of all North Atlantic, Bermuda, Iceland and Russian flights, east of 30 degrees west and north of 5230N. The first Oceanic Controller, F/O Bulstrode RAF sat in the drawing room of Redbrae, with his back to a pleasant sunken garden. In front of him was a large map, where he could chart the progress of early transatlantic deliveries. The Overseas Air Control (OAC) Centre, 44 Group, Gloucester, retained control of aircraft south of 5230N for flights from the UK to Gibraltar/Malta, North Africa and the Middle East. A Search and Rescue Centre for lost and distressed aircraft was also organised. The post-war Oceanic Area Control Centre (OACC) remained at Redbrae House until April 1972.

The Air Ministry had planned two standard hard runways for Prestwick, but in 1940 Scottish Aviation Ltd recommended to Mr J.P. Bickell, the director of ATFERO, that a long and wide main runway would be required for Captain Bennett's tired ferry crews to land on. After heated discussions with the Supply Board of the MAP, Bickell offered his resignation if the recommendation was not met. Work began on a 6,600ft x 300ft runway 14/32 in March 1941. The long and wide runway was completed on 21 September and a second, cross-wind runway 08/26 (4,500ft x 300ft), came into service in May 1942.

Transatlantic Air Control moved into Redbrae House on 6 November 1941 and controlled over 37,000 flights during the Second World War. Following the war, Telecommunications occupied the Redbrae building and Oceanic Control and Scottish Airways were housed in the adjacent Seco huts, until the Ocean moved to Atlantic House in Prestwick in 1972. They were joined by Airways in 1978. (Peter Berry)

A coalition of British, Canadian and American forces was to be found in the Redbrae Trans-Atlantic Air Control Centre. Here on 19 November 1944, Cpl. K.C. Aguirre, USAAF, with a WAAF companion, check Liberator, Fortress and RFS Liberator flights from Canada into Prestwick. (Imperial War Museum, CH.14722)

Return Ferry Service

The return of air-ferry pilots to North America to collect more aircraft had been taking up to six weeks by sea. To speed this up, a Return Ferry Service (RFS) was begun between the UK and Montreal, via Gander, using early production Consolidated LB-30A bombers. The first six LB-30A aircraft off the production line were accepted by the British in December 1940 (AM258-263). With their long range, but lacking self-sealing fuel tanks and turbo-superchargers, these aircraft were modified in Montreal before joining the North Atlantic RFS. The RFS Liberators were flown by BOAC crews, including Captains A.S. Wilcockson, J. Pearcy and O.P. Jones. The first of these Liberators, AM259, arrived at Blackpool/Squires Gate on 14 March 1941, after a flight of 9 hours, 1 minute, followed by two more in April. The first departure of a westbound service from Squires Gate was on 4 May 1941, after being delayed by German bombing, and

Captain D.C.T. Bennett delivered this Consolidated B-24 Liberator I, AM920, from Gander to Prestwick on 13 May 1941, where it joined the BOAC Return Ferry Service. From April to September 1949, it continued in this service, flown by Scottish Airline crews. (Peter M Bowers)

after several return flights the RFS Terminal moved to Prestwick. Meanwhile, the first Consolidated B-24 Liberator I to be delivered to Prestwick, AM912, arrived on 23 April. Liberator AM258 ('9APB') flown by Captain Bennett, arrived at Prestwick from St Hubert, Montreal and Gander on 5 May, after a flight of 19 hours 5 minutes, with four passengers, including Air Marshall Sir Hugh Dowding, on board. Between March and June 1941, an additional nineteen B-24 Liberator Mk.1 bombers (AM910-929) were flown to Prestwick, to be immediately modified by Scottish Aviation for RAF Coastal Command.

Three of these Liberators were added to the Return Ferry Service, being converted by Scottish Aviation with a wooden floor over the bomb-bay and an oxygen system with up to twenty masks for the passengers. From July 1941, regular RFS services were flown six days a week and from 24 September the RFS was operated by BOAC under the AOC RAF Ferry Command. Crew briefing took place in Redbrae, with captains and crews studying weather, diversions, fuel requirements and navigation and communication frequencies. The prototype Curtiss Commando airliner, G-AGDI, was among a number of civil transport aircraft purchased in North America for Britain's wartime routes.

The BOAC RFS flights are recognised as the beginnings of transatlantic landplane passenger air services, which by the end of the war had eclipsed the Foynes, River Shannon to North America services, maintained by the PanAmerican Airlines and BOAC, Boeing 314 Clipper and American Export Sikorsky VS.44A flying-boats.

This BOAC RFS was now to suffer three grievous losses. On 10 August 1941, a Westbound RFS Liberator, AM261, Captain E.R.B. White, having departed from Ayr/Heathfield, crashed into Goat Fell, Isle of Arran, with the

The BOAC Return Ferry Service Consolidated B-24 Liberators had been converted by Scottish Aviation, with sparse accommodation and oxygen for twenty-two ferry crews. Pictured here are a group awaiting take-off in 1941 for the long and cold crossing to Montreal, Canada. (IWM CH.14376)

BOAC Return Ferry Service, Captain J.P. Kirton and crew, receive their transatlantic briefing in the Redbrae Control Centre, before departure for Montreal. (I.W.M. CH.14368)

To bolster the meagre fleet of British transport aircraft, the prototype Curtiss-Wright Commando airliner, NX19436/AC41-21041, was flown from Gander to Prestwick on 12 November 1941. Re-registered G-AGDI and named *St Louis*, it was converted to 24-passenger seats, with the addition of extra fuel tanks. It was flown on long-range routes, as well as along the hazardous Gibraltar-Malta route. (RAF Museum P.5379)

Delivered from Gander to Prestwick on 29/30 December 1941 by Captain D.C.T. Bennett, Lockheed Hudson III, T9465, was marked 'Spirit of Lockheed–Vega Employees', showing that they funded the purchase of the aircraft. It was the last of an initial order for 450 Hudsons for the RAF. (Real Photographs 1835)

Pre-war racing pilot Bob Perlick signs over Consolidated B-24C, Liberator II, AL505, delivered from Gander to Prestwick on 27 September 1941. It was used by the Aircraft & Armament Experimental Establishment, Boscombe Down, for trials. (Imperial War Museum, CH.7357)

loss of twenty-two lives. Four days later, another Liberator, AM260, Captain R.C. Stafford, crashed on take-off from Heathfield, again with the loss of twenty-two lives. There was s third loss on 1 September when an RFS Liberator, AM915, Captain K. Garden, diverting to Squires Gate due to bad weather, hit the top of Achinoan Hill on the Mull of Kintyre. All ten lives were lost.

To house and service the increasing numbers of Hudson and Liberator and Fortress aircraft arriving almost daily, additional hangars were required at SAL and an Air Ministry architect, George G. Baines, proposed the modification of a hangar to a span greater than that of the 120ft wing span of a Liberator, noted on drawings as 'B.1' hangars. Two blocks of three B.1 hangars and a single B.1 were located behind The Palace and two additional B.1 hangars were sited to the north of the large new apron area, now occupied by the SAR Westland Sea King helicopters of HMS Gannet.

Following the early aircraft maintenance and manufacturing work at Prestwick, the year 1942 saw Scottish Aviation busily working on their Supermarine Spitfire repair and sub-contract work, as well as modifications to several marks of Boeing B-17 Flying Fortress, Consolidated B-24 Liberator, Vega B-34 Ventura, Martin B-26 Marauder, Consolidated PBY Catalina, North American B-25 Mitchell, Douglas A-20 Boston and Douglas C-47 Dakota aircraft.

Not all aircraft deliveries were eastbound to Prestwick: on 19 August 1942, Avro Lancaster R5727 was flown to Canada as a pattern aircraft for their manufacture by Victory Aircraft. It returned later in a different guise. By July 1944, the workforce for all activities totalled some 6,500 and the Prestwick factory floor-space had grown from 29,500sq. ft in 1938, to 845,000sq. ft by 1945.

One of the initial eighty-eight, Lockheed Vega B-34, Ventura Mk.I, AE748, was delivered Gander to Prestwick on 16 April 1942. This aircraft served with the Aeroplane & Armament Experimental Establishment and the Empire Central Flying School. (IWM CH.48038)

Flown by pilot/author Don McVicar, Martin B-26A, Marauder I, FK138, was the first for the RAF, arriving at Prestwick from Gander on 2 September 1942. The aircraft served during the war, with No.14 Squadron, RAF, in the Western Desert. (IWM CH.17454)

Only twelve amphibian Consolidated PBY-5A, Catalina Mk.IIIa, were delivered to the RAF. This one, FP529, arrived at Prestwick from Dorval on 9 April 1942. It later flew with No.119 and No.330 (Norwegian) Squadrons and 131 Operational Training Unit. (Imperial War Museum, CH.5948)

Shown in flight, North American B-25B, Mitchell Mk.1, FK161 was delivered to Prestwick from Gander on 20 May 1942. The first for the RAF, she was later flown to the Aeroplane & Armament Experimental Establishment, Boscombe Down, for handling and the writing of the 'pilot's notes'. (Military Aircraft Photographs)

Pictured at the Aeroplane & Armament Experimental Establishment, Boscombe Down, Douglas A-20C, Boston Mk.IIIa, BZ201, was one of three delivered from Reykjavik to Prestwick on 16 November 1942. It later served with No.13 Operational Training Unit at Bicester. (National Archives)

Avro Lancaster Mk.I, R5727, from No.44 (Rhodesia) Squadron, Bomber Command, was flown to Canada from Prestwick on August 19 1942, by round-the-world flyer Clyde Pangborn and his crew. The Lancaster was used as a pattern aircraft for the manufacture of the type in Canada. Once there, it was converted to a Trans-Canada Airline Avro Lancastrian passenger transport and marked CF-CMS, arrived back at Prestwick in July 1943. (IWM. CH.6699)

The United States Army Air Forces Arrive

Even before the United States entered the Second World War, a North Atlantic service was begun by the US Army Corps Ferry Command (ACFC) on 1 July 1941. (From 9 March 1942, the USAAC became the US Army Air Forces, USAAF). Using the Consolidated YB-24 Liberator (AC40-702/'MD120') flown by Lt-Col. Caleb V. Haynes, the survey flight left Washington for the airfield at Ayr/Heathfield. Staging via Montreal, Gander and Reykjavik, they arrived on 3 July, with personnel to assess the requirements for this air route. The return flight was made on 8 July, with a stop at Montreal, arriving back in Washington two days later. A total of twenty return flights were made on this Arnold Line route, named after Col. William W. Arnold of Ferrying Command, before winter conditions suspended operations on 18 October. In addition, YB-24, B-24A AC40-2369 and AC40-2371 to -2376, were flown on the route.

Following the invasion of the Soviet Union by German armed forces on 22 June 1941, two USAAF B-24A Liberator transports (AC40-2371/5), flown by Col. A.J. Harvey and Lt-Col. L.T. Reichers, staged through Prestwick from Washington in September 1941, carrying members of the Harriman Mission to Moscow. A Detachment Eastern Terminus of the North Atlantic Division, US Army Air Corps, was established at Prestwick on 1 October 1941, staffed by military 'Observers' and Commanded by Major J.P.T. Hills.

The first USAAF, Consolidated YB-24 Liberator, to land in wartime Britain was AC40-702, flown by Lt-Col. Caleb V. Haynes, who arrived at Ayr/Heathfield from Washington DC on 3 July 1942. The passengers were 'observers', surveying the air route to Scotland. (The National Archives)

Prestwick was now home to Transatlantic Air Control, the BOAC Return Ferry Service, the 'Arnold' USAAC B-24 Liberator service, No.4 Ferry Pilot Pool of the ATA, No.3 Radio School and the Reception Unit of RAF Ferry Command. No.1527 Blind Approach Training Flight was formed at Prestwick on 29 October 1941, with Oxford and Lockheed Hudson aircraft. The following day, No.1425 Communication Flight was formed with Liberators, to develop long-range ferry services to the Middle East. No.3 Radio School was re-designated No.3 Radio Direction Finding School in August 1942, but soon moved, with their twenty Botha aircraft, to Hooton Park on 1 December.

Contract Carriers

Following the entry of the United States into the war in December 1941 and to provide overseas transport services, the US Government designated several airlines as 'Contract Carriers', including American, American Export, PanAmerican, Trans World Airlines and Northeast Airlines. TWA were the first to establish a transatlantic service from Washington to Prestwick, their Boeing 307 Stratoliner, NC19908 'Apache' arriving from Reykjavik on 18 April 1942. The B307s (later designated C-75s), served the route well, making more than 120 crossings until they were replaced by Douglas C-54A Skymasters on 16 November.

The first transatlantic flight by a C-47 Skytrain (AF41-7833) via Greenland and Iceland (the Northern Route), arrived at Stornoway on 3 July 1942, to deliver a low-frequency Radio Range navigation station. The flight, flown by a Northeast Airlines crew, then continued to Prestwick. On 28 August, the Radio Range station at Prestwick became operational, completing the Army Air Corps Communication System (AACS) 'Airway' across the Northern Route, as good as could be found in the United States. The AACS established a code room and message centre with point-to-point, air/ground, navigation and joint

To bolster the meagre transatlantic passenger capability, four of Trans World Airlines Boeing 307 Stratoliners opened a service from Washington to Prestwick. The first, 'Apache', N-19908, arrived on 18 April 1942. By November, this fleet had completed more than 120 crossings, before being replaced by Douglas C-54A Skymasters. (*The Aeroplane*)

Boeing 307 Stratoliner 'Zuni', N-19907, first arrived at Prestwick on 17 May 1942 and is pictured loading medical cases for evacuation to the United States. Eastbound flights often flew direct from Gander to Prestwick, while westbound flights were routed via Iceland, due to headwinds. (Imperial War Museum, CH.17433)

From October 1942, Douglas C-54A Skymasters began the daily USAAF passenger service across the North Atlantic to Prestwick. Here on the Orangefield Apron are AF41-37289 and AF42-32944. (via Alister Cochrane)

tower control facilities at Prestwick on 1 July. On the 15th, the first land-lines were operational with the British and with the HQ 1st Service Area at USAAF Station 597, Langford Lodge in Northern Ireland, later Base Air Depot No.3.

With bases and facilities ready, a major North Atlantic ferry operation now took place, when Project BOLERO was mounted. Between 23 June and 26 July 1942, forty-nine Boeing B-17E Fortress of the 97th Bomb Group, eighty Lockheed P-38F Lightnings of the 1st Fighter Group and fifty-two Douglas C-47 Skytrains of the 60th Troop Carrier Group were despatched to the 8th Air Force in England from Presque Island, Maine, via the Northern Route to Prestwick. Flown by their combat crews and escorted by B-17 navigation aircraft, five B-17s and six P-38s were lost on the Greenland icecap during the operation, but their crews were saved. Several of these losses were believed to be due to radio bearing interference from a German submarine. The first combat B-17E Flying Fortress to land at Prestwick on 2 July was AF41-9085 'Jarring Jenny'.

A second ferry operation in July 1942 quickly followed the first, under the control of Air Transport Command. Lockheed P-38s from the 14th Fighter Group were escorted by B-17s from the 92nd Bombardment Group (H), USAAF and 301st Bombardment Groups (H) across the North Atlantic without loss, together with C-47s of the 64th Troop Carrier Group. Additional Groups and replacement aircraft for the 8th and 12th Air Forces followed during the remainder of the year, the 2nd Ferrying Group delivering P-38 fighters. The first of these flights were six P-38Gs accompanied by a B-24D 'mother-ship' (AF41-11874). They left New Castle AFB on 5 September, routeing Presque Isle, Maine, Goose Bay, Labrador, BW-1, Greenland, and Reykjavik, Iceland. All arrived at Prestwick on 16 September. The first direct Gander to Prestwick flight by sixteen USAAF B-17 Fortress bombers arrived at Prestwick on 6 September 1942 and the first formation flight of B-24D Liberators of the 93rd Bombardment Group (H) arrived later that month.

Air Transport Command

The first USAAF Air Transport Command unit established at Prestwick was the 31st Ferrying Squadron, made up of men from the 10th AAF, the 2nd Communication and the 15th Air Corps Ferrying Squadrons. The following month, on 7 September 1942, the 53rd Ferrying Squadron was formed at Presque Isle, Maine, becoming part of the 8th Ferrying Group, North Atlantic Wing, ATC. A HQ Squadron, USAAF ATC, was activated at Prestwick and on 1 April 1943 the 8th AFSC and HQ ATC were moved into the second floor of nearby forty-two-roomed Adamton House, assuming command of all USAAF personnel at Prestwick. The 1403 Base Unit was activated on 24 September, with accommodation in Westburn House, adjacent to Redbrae, when all USAAF units at Prestwick were brought under the control of Station 3, ATC.

The USAAF Service and Headquarters, Air Transport Command, moved into the forty-two-roomed Adamton House at Prestwick on 1 April 1943. (Peter Berry)

The USAAF 1403rd Base Unit found accommodation at Westburn House at the airport in September 1943, bringing all USAAF units at Prestwick under the control of Station 3, Air Transport Command. (Peter Berry)

To accommodate the increasing oceanic control operations at the airfield, US Army engineers erected six Seco-huts around the Redbrae Air Traffic Control Centre building on 2 April 1943. These huts continued to house the post-war Oceanic Control Centre until 1972!

From April 1943, Douglas C-54A Skymaster and Consolidated C-87 Liberator transports, operated by TWA from Washington and American Airlines from New York, completed one transatlantic round trip/day to Prestwick. The US Naval Air Transport Service began their Norfolk–Reykjavik–Prestwick service, a Douglas R5D Skymaster, Bu.39137, arriving on 6 May.

A once-only trial was completed on 1 July 1943, when a RAF Dakota, FD900, towing a Waco CG-4 Hadrian glider, FR579 (1-61, 62), arrived at Prestwick, flying in stages across the Northern Route from Dorval, Canada. Trans-Canada Air Lines began a transatlantic service with converted Lancaster aircraft, the first, CF-CMS, arriving at Prestwick on 23 July. Seven Lancastrians were to be converted for this service, which continued until April 1947, when replaced by Canadair DC-4M 'North Stars'.

A once-only transatlantic flight was made in July 1943, by a RAF Douglas Dakota, FD900, towing a Waco CG-4A Hadrian I, glider, FR579, named *Voo-Doo*. Ladened with 3,000lb of military supplies, the Hadrian was towed in stages, from Montreal, Canada to Labrador, then Greenland and Iceland to Prestwick, for a total flight time of 28 hours. (IWM CH.10470 & CH.10472)

Pictured in front of the Orangefield Terminal balcony, Trans-Canada Air Lines Avro Lancastrian, CF-CMS, (ex Lancaster R5727), began passenger services from Montreal to Prestwick in July 1943. (IWM CH.14379)

Scottish Aviation had acquired an old warehouse at 39 West Campbell Street in Glasgow, where the construction of de Havilland DH.82 Queen Bee, radio-controlled target aircraft was sub-contracted to Messrs Morris and the West of Scotland Furniture Co. from Beith. These aircraft were mainly wooden pilot-less versions of the DH Tiger Moth. In August 1943 the first of a contract for 150 aircraft was completed. In November the number was reduced to sixty. The SAL Queen Bees were contained within the serial range, LF779 to LF869. The last Queen Bee was completed and test flown in December 1943. After completion, they were transported to Prestwick airfield, assembled and test flown, before being delivered to the Pilot-less Aircraft Unit (PAU) at Manorbier near St Athan, in south-west Wales, examples being LF789, 'R2-K' and LF801, 'R2-M'. Post-war, as many as forty-three of these aircraft were to be offered for sale!

To enlarge the terminal aircraft control accommodation at the airfield, the civil engineering division of Scottish Aviation was given the task of constructing a modern flying control tower on the pitched roof of the Orangefield Terminal. This was opened for operations on 13 December 1943. Immediately below the tower was the RAF/USAAF, W/T communication centre, together with M/F and H/F D/F bearing and fixing aids and a new Long Range Cathode Ray (LRCR) D/F aid came into service. The terminal reception desk was on the ground floor.

To handle the increasing numbers of aircraft using the airport, a larger control tower and communications centre was opened on the roof of the Orangefield Terminal in December 1943. (Quentin Wilson)

Sergeant A.W. Blake, RAF, from Edgeware, London and his USAAF companion, signal a 'green' from the Orangefield Tower. July 1944 was a busy month, with 8,000 take-offs and landings recorded. (IWM CH.12505)

Sited below the control tower on the roof of the Orangefield Terminal, this Allied radio communications room kept in contact with and provided navigational assistance to arriving flights from North America. (IWM CH.14371)

Sited on the ground floor of the Orangefield Terminal was the reception desk. Here passengers and crew would arrange their overnight accommodation, food and travel arrangements. During the war, some 500,000 persons signed the six registers. The murals over the desk are preserved in the Prestwick Bowling Club. (IWM CH.12510)

To continue the function of wartime air transport of passengers, mail and urgent supplies to the Western Isles, No.1680 Flight had been formed at Abbotsinch in May 1943. The flight moved to Prestwick in March 1944 and continued the service with a variety of transport types, including Dominie, Anson, Dakota and the Fokker F.XXII, G-AFZP, until disbanded in February 1946.

A serious accident occurred on 28 August 1944, when, during an instrument approach to Prestwick, a Douglas C-54A Skymaster AF42-72171, carrying passengers from Stephenville, Newfoundland, collided with a radio mast at the Redbrae Control Centre, crashing into Hillside Avenue, Prestwick. Captain Glen

Golden was killed, together with five crew and fourteen passengers, plus five civilians on the ground.

The Swedish company, ABA, began a Stockholm–Prestwick service carrying passengers and mail, with impressed Boeing B-17 Fortress transports on 10 October 1944, completing eight return flights. The service continued in 1945 and had completed thirty-one return flights up to 9 May. A stop was then added at Gothenburg, Sweden, and weekday flights continued until 2 July, after which the service was routed to London/Croydon Airport.

The RAF Trans-Atlantic Reception Party, which had provided service to 2,662 flights staging through Prestwick, was re-designated the Air Dispatch and Reception Unit in 1944, still within 44 Group. A total of 15,000 transatlantic aircraft had been controlled by the TAC Centre at Prestwick by 22 May that year. Prestwick Tower recorded 7,668 take-offs and landings in July 1944, with 7,847 movements logged in August. To provide final approach guidance in bad weather at Prestwick, 3,000 yards of sodium centre-line lights were laid from the beach to the Runway 14 threshold.

By 7 September 1944, BOAC had flown 1,000 Return Ferry Service flights in their fleet of LB30A/B-24 Liberators. By November, a total of 25,000 wartime transatlantic crossings had been completed, including transport and USAAF and RAF delivery flights. A total of 8,400 aircraft had been delivered to the USAAF in Europe in 1944, including 6,691 by air. Deliveries to the RAF totalled 1,955 in 1944.

The Allied efforts in establishing transatlantic routes and services resulted in 38,044 crossings being controlled by the Trans-Air Control (TAC) at Prestwick, to 31 December 1945. (See Appendix Three).

The airfield at Ayr/Heathfield continued as a RAF fighter base during the war, including a period from April to June 1943, when the 415th Night Fighter Squadron, USAAF, was based there, flying British Bristol Beaufighters. With the lessening threat of German air attack over Scotland, RAF Heathfield was handed to the Royal Navy on 20 October, as HMS *Wagtail*. In addition to the support of disembarked squadrons from Royal Navy aircraft carriers in the Firth of Clyde, the base continued the use of the Fleet Requirements Unit and added No.730 Communication Squadron with Beechcraft Travellers, a Calibration Flight and a Bombardment Spotting School. One of the runways was marked as an aircraft carrier deck and detached squadrons spent hours carrying out Aerodrome Dummy Deck Landing (ADDL) practice.

To recognise their outstanding achievements before and during the war, on 27 June 1945 the Duke of Hamilton and David McIntyre were each given the Freedom of Prestwick.

The Board of Scottish Aviation had proposed to obtain a registered 'Coat of Arms' for the company and this was approved in August, with the words, from Robert Burns, 'The World O'er'.

Opposite top: Together at Prestwick, USAAF Boeing B-17G, AF42-97664 and RAF B-17G Fortress III, HB779, had both landed at Prestwick from Goose Bay, Labrador, on the same day, 6 April 1944. The RAF Fortress served at the Royal Aircraft Establishment, Farnborough and also with No.214 Squadron, carrying out radar countermeasures with No.100 Group. (IWM CH.12504)

Opposite middle: Immediately following their arrival at Prestwick, USAAF crews were met on the apron and given their first words of advice when meeting the local Scots, as well as where the nearest bar and fish and chip shop were located. (IWM (CH.12501)

Opposite bottom: Some 314, Canadian-built Avro Lancaster Mk.X were ferried over the North Atlantic to Prestwick and on to their Squadrons. No serial number is visible on this one, in front of the Orangefield Terminal, but the name 'Laura' graces the door. (via Gordon Macadie)

Above top: A large collection of Lancasters, Liberators, Mosquitos, Mitchells, Skymasters, Fortresses and Spitfires occupy the North East Apron at Prestwick in 1944. (Imperial War Museum, CH.17840)

Above: Shown re-fuelling at Prestwick in 1945, Canadian-built DH.98 Mosquito FB.27 carries its long-range wing drop-tanks and fuselage belly tank, after the 5-hour 15-minute flight across the North Atlantic. Some 437 Mosquitos were delivered to Prestwick. (BAE SYSTEMS)

Douglas C-54D Skymaster Mk.1, KL980, was delivered to Prestwick on 23 March 1945. Flown by the VIP Flight of 246 Squadron, RAF and with KL979, flew Prime Minister Attlee and his party from Northolt to Washington, D.C., in November 1945, to meet President Truman. This Skymaster returned to the US in March 1946 and was assigned to the US Navy as an R5D-3, Bu.91996. (IWM CH.16461)

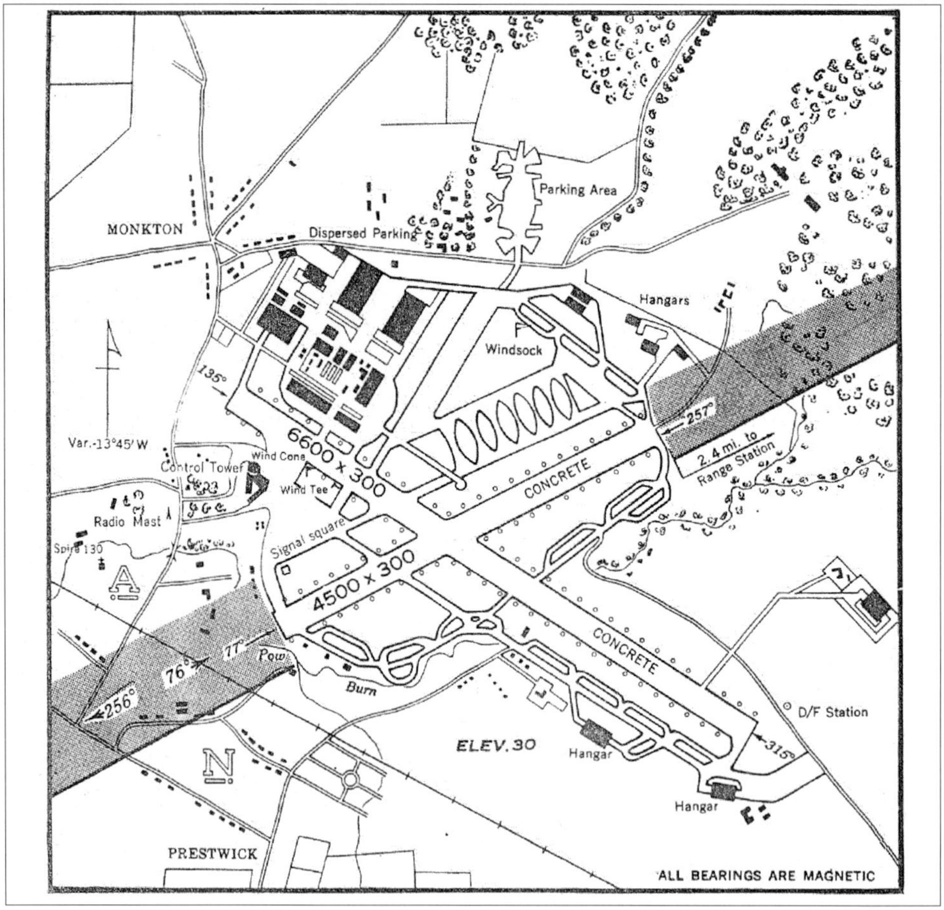

A landing chart for Prestwick, dated January 1945, was issued to crews of North Atlantic Air Transport Command. It shows the Radio Range Approach Aid, aligned along the Prestwick 4,300ft-long, cross-wind Runway 08/26. (USAF)

Pictured on the Ayrshire coast in 1945, Prestwick Airport shows the long and wide Runway 14/32, many aircraft dispersals, the SAL factory buildings and the Isle of Arran in the distance. (via Dougal McIntyre)

Shown here on the Orangefield site at Prestwick Airport, in 1945, is the famous terminal and adjacent service and overnight accommodation buildings. The high radio masts to the left of the picture carried the long-range communication signals to transatlantic aircraft. (via Dougal McIntyre)

The Northeast Apron at Prestwick, shown adjacent to Scottish Aviation in 1945, had spaces for scores of aircraft during the war years and today remains in constant use by civil and military operators. (via Dougal McIntyre)

To show the major contributions achieved at Prestwick during the Second World War, an 'Open Day' was staged at the aerodrome on 15 September 1945 (See Appendix Six).

Military Run-Down

The 1403 Base Unit USAAF at Prestwick had been reduced to a skeleton of personnel by October 1945 and Prestwick ceased to be a terminal for the USAAF Air Transport Command. On 7 October, RAF Transport Command took control of the TAC service and at the end of November 1945 the USAAF returned the Operations Room and accommodation to the British.

An RAF Area Control Centre (ACC) continued at Redbrae to provide service to military aircraft flying over Scotland and a RAF Distress & Diversion Cell (D&D), co-ordinated Search and Rescue services for both military and civil aircraft, replacing the wartime service. The RAF Centre was re-designated as the Prestwick Air Traffic Control Centre (ScATCC (Mil)) in November 1947 and with the onset of the Cold War, an Air Defence Notification Centre (ADNC) was also begun.

Chapter Two

Scottish Aviation Manufacturing, 1945–2004

During the late 1940s, the fluctuating availability of work for SAL caused concern. In January 1944, David McIntyre again visited Consolidated Aircraft on the west coast of the United States and gained approval for

Shown in 1946, the Scottish Aviation factory site and large aircraft apron area dominate the area around Monkton village. (BAE SYSTEMS)

modifications to the Liberator, should SAL decide to build a new civil transport version. They then supplied a small number of conversions of the wartime Liberator bomber to 24-seat civil transports. McIntyre also signed a Letter of Agreement with TWA, should Scottish Airlines begin transatlantic air services.

SAL also gained a licence agreement with the Douglas Aircraft Co. to consolidate its wartime role as the design authority for the repair, overhaul and conversion of Douglas C-47/DC-3 Dakota and Douglas C-54/DC-4 Skymaster aircraft to civil transports. With these agreements and their wartime expertise in overhauling Dakota and Liberator transports, SAL was soon into the business of converting ex-RAF machines for the emerging post-war airlines. A first order for five conversions to Douglas DC-3 standard, PH-TBR, came from Royal Dutch Airlines (KLM), to be followed by many more. The first Portuguese DC-3 for Transportes Aereos Portugueses (TAP), CS-TDF, was completed in 1946, followed by HB-IRL, to Swissair and LN-NAD, to Fred Olsen Air Transport. Other conversions were for Aer Lingus, TWA and AOA in the United States, TAP in Portugal, SABENA in Belgium, and Airlines in Norway and Denmark, before they amalgamated into the Scandinavian Airline System (SAS).

Further afield, there were conversions for the airlines of Ceylon, Cyprus, Abyssinisa, Bharat, Orient Airways in Pakistan, Olympic Airways and Hellenic Airlines and the airlines of Luxembourg, Iceland, Czechoslovakia, Algeria, Syria and several charter airlines, including Channel, Jersey, Westminster, Global, Blue Sky and Alpar SA. In total, nearly 300 DC-3 and DC-4 transports were converted for civil use. In December 1945, SAL also acquired the rights for the overhaul of Pratt & Whitney aero engines and instruments made by the Sperry Gyroscope Co. A 75 per cent stake to market the Bell 47 helicopter in August 1947 resulted in several being imported and flown by Scottish Aviation's Chief Test Pilot, J Noel 'Cap' Capper. The venture was not a success.

The lean manufacturing times of 1947 saw Scottish Aviation diversifying into non-aviation markets. First was the production of light-alloy tractor cabs, followed by single and double-decker bus bodies. Mr T.D.M. Robertson from Hawker Aircraft at Kingston was chosen as the new G.M. of Design, Administration and Manufacturing at Scottish Aviation. He soon identified the non-profit-making work and from July 1950 cleared space for the conversion of the thirty-eight wartime Dakota aircraft, to the 32-seat 'Pionair' Class for British European Airways (BEA). He also secured orders for rudders from A.V. Roe for their contract for Canberra jet bombers, as well as the overhaul of engines from Rolls-Royce and de Havillands.

Prestwick Pioneer

In February 1945, Scottish Aviation submitted a design study to meet Air Ministry Specification A.4/45. This was for a light, 3-seat cabin, high-wing monoplane for communication with officers in the field. The aircraft was to be of robust construction and suitable for landing on rough surfaces and small landing grounds. Design work began and on 5 November 1947 the prototype Pioneer (VL515) was first flown, powered by a 240hp DH Gipsy Queen engine. Converted to a 4-seat aircraft and powered by a 520hp Alvis Leonides engine, the Pioneer series 2 aircraft was flown on 5 May 1950/G-AKBF/G-31-1). A total of fifty-nine Pioneers were sold to the RAF as well as the Ceylonese and Malaysian Air Forces. The first Pioneer was delivered to the RAF in September 1953 (VL516/G-ANAF/XE514). The RAF Pioneers were to see much service in the jungles of Malaya during unrest in 1954/55 and were not withdrawn until 1968.

Designed as a light military transport aircraft with short take-off and landing capability, the DH Gipsy-powered, Scottish Aviation Prestwick Pioneer, VL515, was first flown in November 1947. Marked G-31-1, the prototype was flown at the SBAC display at Farnborough in 1948. Found to be under-powered, the prototype was re-engined as the Pioneer 2. (via Dougal McIntyre)

Fitted with the more powerful 520hp Alvis Leonides engine, the Scottish Aviation Pioneer 2, G-ANAZ, was first flown on 3 September 1953, appearing at that year's Farnborough Air Show. This aircraft was converted to an RAF Pioneer CC.1, marked XE514, and served with No.267 Squadron in Malaya. (Peter Berry)

Prestwick Twin Pioneer

A larger, twin-engine design, the 16-seat, followed and was first flown on 25 July 1955 (G-ANTP). A Certificate of Airworthiness was issued in November 1956, and the first aircraft of an order for thirty-nine for the RAF, (XL966), was flown on 29 August 1957.

The grievous loss of David McIntyre and his crew following a structural failure on 7 December 1957 during a demonstration tour with the Twin Pioneer, G-AOEO, in North Africa was a blow to the future expectations of Scottish Aviation. However, the company responded with a new vigour and worked hard to continue the vision of the past twenty-two years. After modification, production continued and a variety of civil operators purchased the remainder of the eighty-seven Twin Pioneers to be built, the last in 1962.

The prototype Scottish Aviation Twin Pioneer, G-ANTP, was first flown on 25 June 1955. Displayed at SBAC Farnborough later that year, a contract for thirty-nine from the RAF ensured a production run of eighty-seven, including those for the Royal Malaysian Air Force. (Peter Berry)

Pictured in Borneo Airway markings, over the Scottish Aviation factory at Prestwick in 1955, Twin Pioneer VR-OAE was later flown by Kuwait Airways. (via Gordon Macadie)

Scottish Aviation Military Contracts

From 1953, pending delivery of the anti-submarine, Fairey Gannet, Scottish Aviation modified some 100 US Navy Grumman TBM Avengers, as Mk.AS.4 and 5 aircraft for the Royal Navy.

In November 1954, SAL began a series of aircraft maintenance contracts for the RCAF European 1st Aircraft Division at their site at Renfrew Airport. At first, the aircraft overhauled were the Douglas C-47 Dakotas and Beechcraft C-45 Expeditors, soon followed by Canadair CF-100 Canuck and Canadair Sabre jet-fighters, together with Canadair T-33AN Silver Star trainers. In the summer of 1960 this work was transferred to Prestwick and there soon followed, from January 1963, a contract for the maintenance and overhaul of Canadair CF-104 Starfighters. The 1,000th completion was in December 1967 and these contracts were closed in 1978.

Parked among the hangars at SAL in 1968, this RCAF Douglas Dakota 661 was restored the following year for the Royal Aircraft Establishment, West Freugh, Scotland, as 'KG661' and named *Portpatrick Princess*. In 1979, the marking was found to be in error and was changed to ZA947. The Dakota survives today with the RAF Battle of Britain Memorial Flight. (Peter Berry)

Four squadrons of Canadian Air Force, Avro Canada CF.100 Canuck fighter aircraft, were based in Europe in the 1960s, including this one, RCAF 18344, being serviced and modified by Scottish Aviation at Prestwick. (Gordon Macadie)

From 1960, many Orenda-powered, Canadair CL-13B Sabre Mk.6 from the eight squadrons of the RCAF serving in Europe, were serviced and modified by Scottish Aviation at Prestwick, including this one, RCAF23499, coded 'TF', (Gordon Macadie)

Shown at Prestwick in 1970, this Canadair F-104G Starfighter, 104862, is about to depart on a test flight, with resident Canadian Air Force test pilot, Mark Fairlie. (Gordon Macadie)

A two-seat, Canadair F-104D, 104634, was sometimes used to return squadron pilots to their bases in Europe, after they had delivered single-seat Starfighters to Prestwick for overhaul. (Gordon Macadie)

The Silver Jubilee of Scottish Aviation in 1960 saw the company in much better shape, with diversification of work and with some important contracts to come. A new, large 'Britannia' hangar of 45,000ft was built in 1965, to provide adequate space for the maintenance of Laker Britannia and Loftleider CL-44s, as well as overhaul and conversion work for a wide range of aircraft types, including the fitting of cargo doors to Aer Lingus Viscounts. 'SAL Check' was formed in June 1962, as an approved aircraft overhaul, repair and maintenance service and was to continue in operation for many years. Also in 1962, twelve Fleet Air Arm Skyraider aircraft were converted as target-tugs for the Swedish Air Force. Two Convairliner 440 transports, N7262 and N7263, purchased by General Dynamics from Aramco, were converted by SAL in 1966, to Model 640, with the fitting of Rolls-Royce Dart turbo-props. By 1968, the department had handled a total of 566 aircraft maintenance contracts.

Rolls-Royce Merlin and Griffon aero engines were added to the engine overhaul business. Scottish Air Engine Services were housed in the pre-war 'Tiger' hangar. By 1966, SAL had taken over all maintenance work of Rolls-Royce piston engines and when this work finally came to an end in 1981, SAES had overhauled 1,910 Griffon engines.

Scottish Aviation gained a contract in 1966 to manufacture 20ft-long centre-panel sections for the Lockheed C-130 Hercules military transport, as well as the under-wing fuel tank pylons. The Hercules work was sited in the pre-war

Shown inside the large Britannia Hangar at Prestwick, Canadair CL44J, TF-LLH, was named *Gudridur Thorbjarnardottir*, of Loftleidir Air Lines, and is seen undergoing routine maintenance at Prestwick. (BAE SYSTEMS)

Running up her inner engine, Lockheed L-749A, G-ASYF of Ace Scotland, was at Scottish Aviation in January 1966, for conversion to a 82-seat Inclusive Tour interior. Following the summer season, the airline ceased operations and the aircraft was stored at Coventry/Baginton. (W. Stevenson)

Fokker Hangar and on completion of the contract in 1982, 773 ship sets of C-130 fuselage panels had been dispatched to Lockheed. Doors for the Lockheed Tristar were another source of work and more recently, the jet engine pylons for the BAe.146.

In April 1966, it was announced that Scottish Aviation had been taken over by the ship-builder's Cammell Laird. With a declining ship-building market, the company was diversifying into other fields.

Handley Page Jetstream

The Cammell Laird take-over of Scottish Aviation in 1966 allowed the investment in a far-reaching project. Handley Page was developing their small, twin-engine 18-seat airliner and required a sub-contractor to manufacture the wing sets. SAL were successful in this tender and received a contract to produce fifty-four sets of wings, following on from the last of the Twin Pioneers, the first two being delivered in October 1967. The first Astazou-powered Jetstream flew at Radlett on 18 August 1967 (G-ATXH). This construction programme became too much for the financial base of Handley Page and the company was forced into receivership on 7 August 1969. Some forty Handley Page Jetstreams had flown. Jetstream wing production ceased at Prestwick on 27 February 1970 and in April, Handley Page went into liquidation.

Captain Bill Bright of Terravia acquired the rights and much hardware, as Jetstream Aircraft Limited, including the prototype of a Garrett-engine C-10A transport prototype, intended to replace the USAF Convair T-29A. This prototype, G-AWBR, had flown on 21 November 1968. With the resulting payment difficulties from Handley Page and indeed the collapse of Rolls-Royce at this time, Cammell Laird/Scottish Aviation was left in a perilous position. The saving grace for Scottish Aviation at Prestwick came from another failure in the British aircraft industry.

Bulldog Trainer

Beagle Aircraft had developed a successor to the early Beagle Pup light trainer and had secured an order for fifty-eight Bulldogs from the Royal Swedish Air Force. The first Bulldog trainer, converted from a Pup, had made its first flight on 19 May 1969 (G-AXEH), but flight tests were not completed as Beagle went into receivership in early 1970. The British Government accepted responsibility for the Swedish Contract and then gave Scottish Aviation a contract to build these aircraft. Scottish Aviation also continued to support the other Beagle designs, the Pup, Basset and Beagle 206.

The production team at Prestwick went to work on the new design and the second prototype was moved to Prestwick for completion. It was first flown on 14 February 1971 (G-AXIG). The first production Bulldog was flown on 21 June 1971 (G-AYWN/Swedish 61001) and was delivered on the 26th of the following month.

SAL went on to build ninety Bulldog Trainers for the Sweden Army and Air Force. This was followed by orders for 132 more for the RAF, to replace the Chipmunk basic trainer, as well as orders from Malaysia, Kenya, Ghana, Nigeria, Jordan, Lebanon, Hong Kong and Botswana, for a total of 324 Bulldogs. Many Bulldogs are now finding a ready sale in the civilian market.

Shown on a test flight from Prestwick, Scottish Aviation Bulldog FM1233, was one of fifteen supplied to the Royal Malaysian Air Force in 1972. (via Dougal McIntyre)

The first flight of a vintage Klemm L.25a, G-AAUP, was made on 31 May 1972, after a long restoration by SAL engineer, Bob Russell. The Klemm, the oldest flying aircraft in Scotland at that time, graced many Air Shows during the following years.

Military Jetstreams

In 1970, the RAF had stated a requirement for a multi-engine training aircraft to replace the ageing Vickers Varsity. Scottish Aviation tendered for a Ministry of Defence contract, along with Captain Bill Bright, on the basis that SAL would acquire the assets for the Jetstream, if the tender was successful. On 24 February 1972, the Government awarded Scottish Aviation the contract for twenty-six aircraft (later twenty-eight), for the Royal Air Force. Scottish Aviation had fifteen sets of completed wings, with seven more in assembly. The tail unit of the Jetstream was already under sub-contract to North West Industries of Canada. Three Handley Page-built fuselages were completed and a further eleven were in storage. In addition, seven fuselages were partly completed, which left Scottish Aviation needing five new fuselages to complete the contract. After looking for a sub-contractor for this work, SAL decided to set up their own production line for these fuselages and they completed the contract, the last RAF Jetstream T.1, XX500 being flown in December 1976.

The first two aircraft were restored from Jetstreams returned from the United States. On Friday 13 April 1973, the first of twenty-six Astazou-powered Jetstream T.1 for the RAF was flown (XX475) and was delivered on 26 June. To delay the delivery of the contract, it was agreed that the last ten aircraft would be for civil use, followed by ten new aircraft for the RAF. In October 1976, Scottish Aviation AL began a contract to convert sixteen of the RAF Jetstreams as T.2,

A Klemm L.25a sporting monoplane G-AAUP was built in Germany in 1929 as a company demonstrator. It was restored by a SAL engineer, Bob Russell, and flown at Prestwick in May 1972. At that time, it was the oldest airworthy aeroplane in Scotland. (Peter Berry)

for the Fleet Air Arm Observer School at 750 Squadron RN Culdrose. Two further T.2 were added in 1982/83. The ten RAF T.1s retired on 19 March 2004, XX496 being flown to join the Scottish Aviation Pioneer and Twin Pioneer at the RAF Museum, Cosford. (See Appendix Eleven)

Scottish Aviation to British Aerospace

The Labour victory in the General Election of 1974, led to the amalgamation and nationalisation of most of the units of the British aircraft industry. At first Laird/Scottish Aviation were excluded, due to their lower financial turnover, but following representations to the Government, on 1 January 1978, Scottish Aviation became a division of British Aerospace.

BAE Jetstream

Before Nationalisation, the SAL Board had considered the development of the Garrett-powered Jetstream. The power-plant of the fifty-seven Astazou Jetstreams in service had received criticism, particularly in the United States, where some airframes had already been converted to Garrett turboprops. Since the first design of the Jetstream, 'de-regulation' had allowed regional airline operators to fly passengers into the large 'hub' airports. To achieve this they required a pressurised, modern, Jetstream-sized transport.

A new Nationalised British Aerospace gave approval for the development of the Jetstream 31 in January 1981 and an early Handley Page 200 series airframe was purchased from the Unites States (N510F). This was used as a development aircraft. The Garrett-powered, prototype Jetstream 31 G-JSSD, was first flown on 28 March 1980. The first production Jetstream 31 was flown on 18 March 1982 (G-TALL) and was awarded a Certificate of Airworthiness on 29 July. An American Approved Type Certificate followed on 1 December. More than 100 Jetstreams had been sold by August 1985, 85 to North America. Some 386 Jetstreams 31/32 had been delivered when production ceased in 1997.

In November 1989, design work began on a longer 29-seat, Jetstream 41 version. When first flown on 25 September 1991 this model (G-GCJL) had attracted twenty-six orders. The CofA was granted on 23 November 1992. British Aerospace announced in June 1997 that Jetstream production would be completed at the end of the year. This was due to the state of world markets and competition from some foreign manufacturers enjoying a subsidy from their State. A total of 103 Jetstream 41s were completed, the last departing Prestwick on 26 March 1998. Later in the year, two Jetstream 41s were delivered to the Hong Kong Government with the addition of a ventral radar dome and internal equipment for the Maritime Reconnaissance and Air Sea Rescue role.

Shown formatting along the Ayrshire Coast, BAe Jetstream 31, G-BTXG, is joined by Jetstream 41, G-JMAC. The latter aircraft is now displayed outside the Marriott Hotel, Liverpool Airport. (BAE SYSTEMS)

British Aerospace Flying College

A British Aerospace Flying College began flight operations at Prestwick on 20 May 1988. The fleet of training aircraft included twelve FFA AS.202 Bravo, thirty Piper Cherokee and ten Piper Senecas. The college was formally opened on 24 November and the fleet of training aircraft was housed in the refurbished, pre-war Fokker Hangar. Adamton House, with additional bedrooms for 250 student pilots, was used for their accommodation. Due to the increasing commercial flights at Prestwick, training flights in the Prestwick circuit began to be restrictive and by 1999 the college had closed and moved to a new location in Seville.

British Aerospace celebrated twenty-one years of operation at Prestwick in April, 1998. General Manager Tom Williams, reported that 1,000 employees were now concentrating on supporting the Twin Pioneer, Bulldog and Jetstream operators as well as manufacturing parts for a number of military and civil aircraft.

Today, a Regional Aircraft Division of BAE SYSTEMS at Prestwick supports the continued operation of the BAe.146 four-jet transports, the Avro turbo-prop airliners, as well as the Jetstream fleet. Engineers are now engaged on conversion programmes, such as the Atmospheric Research aircraft and fire-bomber versions of the BAe.146, as well as the design and systems for the new RAF BAe. Nimrod ocean-patrol aircraft. An Aerostructures Division continues the manufacture of aircraft components for Airbus, Boeing and the Hawker 125 business jet.

The British Aerospace Flight Training School opened in 1988. It was accommodated in the pre-war 'Fokker' Hangar at Prestwick Airport. Their fleet of Piper Cherokee, FFA Bravo and Piper Seneca aircraft were also housed within this hangar. (Peter Berry)

Looking across Prestwick Airport to the south-west in 1999, the factory complex of BAE SYSTEMS dominates the north side of Runway 13. (PIK)

Chapter Three

Post-War Developments, 1946–2004

During 1942 and 1943, several schemes were proposed by SAL to the Director-General of Civil Aviation, Air Ministry, for a Target Plan for the development of Prestwick as a post-war transatlantic airport. These plans included new long runways and a flying-boat base adjacent to the airport. Support came from the Clyde Navigation Trust, the Scottish Council on Industry and Ayr County Council. In October 1945, a deputation, including Sir Steven Bilsland and Bailie Elger for the Scottish Council on Industry, with the Duke of Hamilton, Carlyle Gifford, David McIntyre and the Earl of Selkirk, for Scottish Aviation, met the Minister of Civil Aviation, Lord Winster, at Aerial House in London. He was able to tell them that it was now agreed that Prestwick Airport should be designated as an international airport and should also be the bad-weather alternative airport for Heathrow. No operator should be discouraged from using Prestwick as an international airport terminal and that serious consideration should be given to the development of ancillary services at Prestwick

Following the Nationalisation of the airlines and airports, a compulsory acquisition order for the Prestwick site was served by the Ministry of Civil Aviation (MCA) on 1 April 1946, who purchased the airport holding of Scottish Aviation Ltd (SAL). Prestwick had, however, been designated as the second International Airport with London's recently opened airport at Heathrow the first. The Orangefield Hotel/Tower became the civil passenger terminal at the airport, operated by Scottish Aviation Ltd. The Royal Air Force handed the tower, approach control and Transatlantic Air Control to the MCA on 1 May and Transatlantic Air Control (TAC), became the Oceanic Area Control Centre (OACC) at Prestwick. Together with Shannon, 'Shanwick Control' was responsible for co-ordinating ATC clearances to departing and arriving flights

This picture of Prestwick Airport, looking east in 1950, shows the Scottish Aviation factory complex on the left and the Orangefield Terminal and Tower Control Site on the right. At the bottom of the picture, the Ayr to Monkton and Kilmarnock road can be seen, soon to be crossed by the extension of Runway 14. (via Gordon Macadie)

through their national airspace, terminating at 30 degrees west. En route oceanic re-clearances involved co-ordination between each centre. The introduction of these operating procedures was delayed until 1 November 1946.

The increasing size of civil and military aircraft using Prestwick found the length of the original crosswind Runway 08/26 too short and discussion took place with the Air Ministry during 1947 with regard to bringing in a second runway. The Air Ministry favoured an extension to 13/31, with a North South runway between Monkton village and its local railway station. In the event, Runway 03/21 (6,000ft by 240ft) was aligned from the end of the 31 touchdown area, to within a short distance of the runways at Ayr/Heathfield, coming into service on 3 September 1955. This allowed the Local Authority to move forward with their housing schemes, now completed around the East Road in Prestwick.

Adamton House was purchased in 1947 by the MCA and housed the Scottish Divisional Headquarters until purchased by the BAA plc in April 1971. The MCA took over all the airport buildings from SAL, except the Orangefield Terminal, and from 1 April 1948, the MCA took over the aircraft handling services from Scottish Aviation. To ensure adequate instrument approach guidance to Britain's major airports, American surplus Ground Controlled Approach (GCA) units were acquired by the MCA and were introduced at London Airport on 1 July 1947, at Prestwick on 1 January 1948 and at Liverpool/Speke on 18 May the same year.

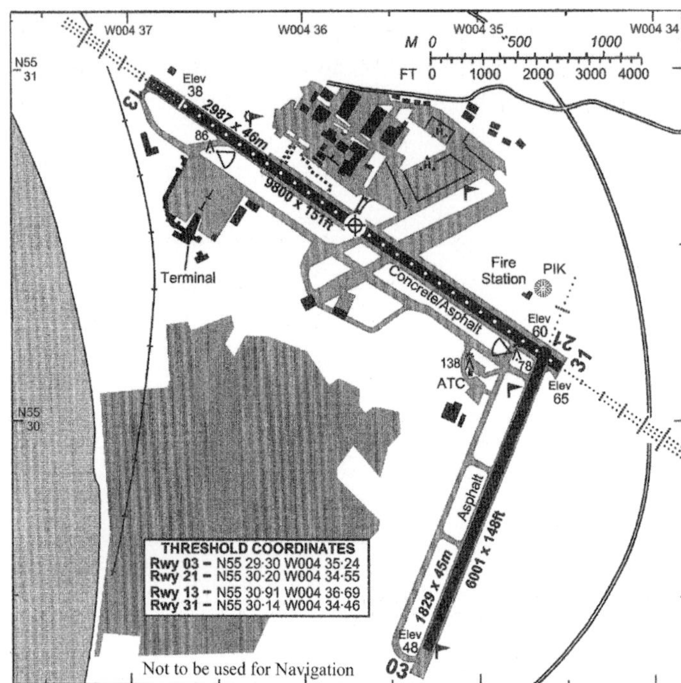

This Landing Chart for Prestwick, dated 2004, shows that Runway 08/26 is out of use and Runway 13 covers the Prestwick to Monkton main road, which has been replaced by a dual carriageway. A new terminal, control tower and parallel taxiway are shown, together with the A77, dual carriageway to the east of the airport. (AERAD)

Re-surfacing of the runways at Prestwick took place in 1949 and to lengthen the take-off distance 1,000ft of grass overrun was added to the re-designated Runway 13/31 in 1952 for a total of 7,600ft. February 1950 saw the return of G.J.H. Jeffs, OBE, as Airport Commandant, who had witnessed the Monkton landing ground of 1933 and managed the Orangefield Terminal from 1940.

The deepening of the Cold War in the 1950s and '60s saw the 1,631st Air Base Group activated at Prestwick in November 1951 to handle US Military Air Transport Service (MATS) flights between the United States and Europe, and building works began on the disused aircraft dispersal sites on the north-east side of the airport, to be known as the 'Greensite'. This facility provided full aircraft maintenance facilities and accommodation for USAF personnel. From 18 May 1952 the USAF based the 67th Air Rescue Squadron at Prestwick, using the new Greensite facility to the north-east of the airport, with additional passenger transit accommodation available in the Orangefield Terminal. During these years, the terminal returned to its wartime role as a haven for visiting American military personnel and their families. The first transatlantic crossing by helicopters was completed in July 1952, when two Sikorsky H-19 helicopters of the USAF, AF51-3983, 'Hopalong', and AF51-3894, 'Whirlaway', arrived at Prestwick from Reykjavik.

From October 1953 the Squadron began operations from Prestwick, initially operating SB-17H Fortress aircraft; the SB-29 Superfortress followed and in 1954 so did Grumman SA-16 Albatross amphibians, and later the Douglas SC-54 Skymaster and Lockheed HC-130H Hercules.

A major USAF accident occurred on 14 December 1953, when one of the Boeing SB-29 Superfortress Rescue aircraft (AF44-86308) on a training exercise from Prestwick and carrying an airborne lifeboat, reported a runaway propeller, which then broke off, slashing the right-hand side of the fuselage. An emergency landing was made on Runway 31, without the main gear being down, squashing the lifeboat under the belly. No fatalities were reported.

Since the requisition of the Prestwick site by the RAF in 1941 and the compulsory acquisition of Prestwick Airport by the Ministry of Civil Aviation (MCA) in 1946, Scottish Aviation spent many years of meetings and litigation to recover rent due, as well as compensation for the compulsory acquisition of their

Serving with the 67th Air Rescue Squadron, USAF, in 1960, Grumman SA-16B amphibian, AF51-5287, is shown at Prestwick during a USAF 'Open House'. (Gordon Macadie)

On display at a Prestwick 'Open House' in 1965, Lockheed HC-130H Hercules, AF65-952, was assigned to the USAF 67th Air Rescue Squadron. A rare Douglas HC-54G Skymaster, AF45-608, hides behind. (Cyril Lofthouse)

A major USAF accident occurred on 14 December 1953 at Prestwick, when one of the Boeing SB-29 Superfortress aircraft (AF44-86308), from the 67th Air Rescue Squadron, carrying an airborne lifeboat, reported damage following a runaway propeller. An emergency landing was made on Runway 31, squashing the lifeboat under the belly. No fatalities were reported. (via Alisdair Cochrane)

assets. It was not until 1953 that a settlement was reached and Scottish Aviation was granted a lease for ninety-nine years on their site.

With the threat of the Cold War continuing, the USAF Military Air Transport Service assigned the 1,602nd Air Transport Wing to Prestwick in 1956, to support the 1,631st Air Base Group and their assigned 67th Air Rescue Squadron, USAF and Detachments of the 18th Weather and 3rd Postal Squadrons, together with the 1,276th Airways and Air Communications Service (AACS) Squadron. Military Air Transport Service (MATS) also opened an operation and passenger terminal, to handle the many military passengers in transit to Europe. A Douglas VC-47D Skytrain AF45-1057 was the base aircraft during these years. The historic Adamton House, east of the airfield, was again occupied by the USAF, this time as the officer's club.

In addition to the Boeing WB-50D weather reporters, Boeing KB-50J Superfortress tankers became regular visitors to Prestwick; also large formations of single-engine jet fighter aircraft in transit, to be delivered to bases in Europe, would be parked at Prestwick. A stream of Douglas C-54 Skymaster, Douglas C-118 Liftmaster, Boeing C-97G Stratofreighters, Lockheed C-130A and C-130E Hercules, Douglas C-124A Globemasters, Lockheed EC-121 Constellations, Douglas C-133A Cargomasters, Lockheed C-141 Starlifters and Lockheed C-5A Galaxy transports supported these movements. A rare sight in 1961 was a major USAF/MATS logistics Cold War 'Biglift' exercise, which resulted in more than forty Douglas C-118A 'Liftmaster' transports being parked on the north-east apron. The US Navy was well represented too, with Douglas C-117D Super conversions of the R4D-8 Skytrain, Douglas R5D Skymasters, Lockheed P2V Neptunes, together with early warning WV-2 versions of the Lockheed WV-2 Constellation. Later, several marks of Lockheed P-3 Orions were frequent visitors.

Providing the USAF and her Allies with accurate weather information, this Boeing WB-50D Superfortress, AF49-273, from the 53rd Weather Reconnaissance Squadron, Burtonwood, is shown in transit at Prestwick in 1959. (via Gordon Macadie)

Parked at the USAF Greensite base at Prestwick during a USAF 'Open House' in 1961, Boeing KB-50J aerial tanker, AF48-094, was from the 420th Air Refuelling Squadron, based at Sculthorpe. It has a J47-GE jet engine under each wing, for extra boost when refuelling jet-powered bombers and fighters. (Gordon Macadie)

During the build-up of Allied forces during the Cold War, the USAF flew formations of fighter aircraft into Europe. More than thirty are seen here at Prestwick in 1952, including Republic F-84D Thunderjet, AF48-731. (via Gordon Macadie)

Shown landing on Runway 13 at Prestwick, Douglas VC-54E Skymaster, AF44-9045, had seen service in the Pacific War Zone and in 1945 carried the Japanese envoys to Manila, in the Philippines, during the surrender negotiations. (Gordon Macadie)

Seen departing Runway 31 at Prestwick, Douglas C-118A AF53-3280, Liftmaster, was one of many in transit during the mid-1950s and '60s. (Gordon Macadie)

Climbing out past the Orangefield Terminal in April 1965, USAF Rescue Boeing HC-97G Stratofreighter, AF53-117, was based at Prestwick, pending the transition from the Douglas HC-54D to the Lockheed HC-130A. (W. Stevenson)

A USAF, Lockheed RC-130A, 57-516, shown taxying past the remaining pre-war Watch Tower at Prestwick in 1965 was from the 1,370th Photo Mapping Wing of the Military Air Transport Service. (Gordon Macadie)

Shown departing Runway 31 at Prestwick in 1961, Douglas C-124C Globemaster II transport, AF52-1011, was bound for the Lajes AFB in the Azores. (Gordon Macadie)

Lockheed EC-121H Constellation, AF55-131, shown at the USAF Greensite at Prestwick, in 1966, was tasked during the Cold War with distant Airborne Early Warning and Counter Weapons over the oceans and sparely populated territories. (Gordon Macadie)

Douglas C-133A Cargomaster, AF54-135, a diversion to Prestwick in 1961, was the first aircraft off the production line and served with the 39th Transport Squadron of MATS. The type suffered from turbo-prop engine problems. (Gordon Macadie)

A fleet of 285, Lockheed C-141B Starlifters, replaced the earlier USAF MATS, C-97, C-118 and C-121 strategic military transports. This one, AF66-7956, is seen taxying for departure at Prestwick in June 1985. (Peter Berry)

The USAF MATS heavy lift cargo transport, the Lockheed C-5A Galaxy, has seen service during recent conflicts in Europe and the Middle East. AF70-460 is seen departing Runway 13 at Prestwick in July 1989. (Peter Berry)

Based at RAF Mildenhall, US Navy Douglas C-117D, Bu.17191, was a frequent visitor to Prestwick in the 1970s. Following retirement, she was flown to Keflavik in Iceland and was displayed at the Naval Air Station. (Gordon Macadie)

In transit at Prestwick in 1963, Lockheed EC-121K, Constellation, Bu.128324, named *Sundowner* and painted in Day-Glo trim, is marked 'W'. It had been used for Weapon System Tests at the US Naval facility at Patuxent River, Maryland. (Gordon Macadie)

New Terminal Building and ATC Tower Announced

In the early 1960s plans were announced for a £4 million upgrade to Runway 13/31 and improved passenger facilities at the airport. A new parking apron with twelve jet aircraft stands was built in front of a new passenger terminal and a well-placed new control tower was to be sited at the intersection of the two main runways. A new fire station was also planned. To accept the turbo-jet traffic of the five transatlantic operators using Prestwick, BOAC, Scandinavian Airlines System, KLM Dutch Airlines, PanAmerican and Trans-Canada Air Lines, Runway 13/31 was lengthened to 9,800ft and opened on 17 May 1960. This extension was to cause distress to motorists, due to the closing of the Ayr–Glasgow road when take-offs and landings were taking place. A new dual carriageway was completed to the west of the new terminal building in 1964, to resolve these delays.

Pictured shortly after the opening of the new terminal building at Prestwick in 1964, the new boundary dual-carriageway road is shown, with the apron area awaiting the completion of the parallel taxi-track. (via Dougal McIntyre)

Well sited at the intersection of Runways 13/31 and 03/21 at Prestwick, the control tower was opened in 1964. (Peter Berry)

Prestwick had always been the most fog-free airport in the country and this diversion status for civil and military aircraft continues to this day. Prestwick was also the first airport in the UK to offer duty-free purchases, from March 1959, and attracted as many as 62,000 sightseers in 1962. Construction of a new terminal building and control tower began in June 1961, and the control tower was opened on 24 April 1962, at the intersection of Runways 13/31 and 03/21. The new terminal building, with a two-level 'finger', was opened by HM Queen Mother on 22 September 1964. A proposed covered link to a new station on the adjacent Stranraer–Glasgow railway line was not completed until 1994. A proposed modern transit hotel was never built. As part of the re-development work at the airport, from 1960, the Tiger and Anson Hangars were removed to increase clearance from Runway 13/31. In the summer of 1964, the MCA installed an emergency arrester gear at the west end of Runway 31 to stop any Canadian CF-104 jet-fighters over-running the runway after their maintenance test flights.

In June 1966, the USAF and 67th Air Rescue Squadron, equipped with HC-130 aircraft, left the Greensite at Prestwick and was re-located to the Moron AFB in Spain, to cover the increasing number of nuclear deterrent aircraft stationed in Europe. As a result of this closure, MATS, now named Military Airlift Command (MAC), moved their passenger handling offices to the new terminal building at Prestwick, along with elements of the US Navy. The Greensite area, maintenance and accommodation facilities were taken over by the Royal Navy and commissioned as 'HMS Gannet' on 23 November 1970. The Military Airlift Command Terminal handling of US Navy Polaris crews and families from the Holy Loch continued at Prestwick until the last civilian charter flight departed on 31 March 1992.

Prestwick Airport Future

During the 1960s, the future role of Prestwick Airport was raised in discussions between local business interests and the British Airports Authority. The recent Bermuda 2 Agreement between Britain and the United States included the recognition of Prestwick as the designated International Gateway to Scotland, for scheduled and charter air services.

Orangefield Terminal Demolished

The historic Orangefield Terminal and most of the surrounding buildings were demolished in 1966/67 to provide a clear access for the construction of the remaining section of the parallel taxi-track to the south of Runway 13/31. It was completed some three years later.

The location of Prestwick close to the preferred Great Circle, North Atlantic routes to Iceland and North America, has been the catalyst for the re-fuelling stops for many aircraft being delivered in both east and west directions. The first commercial turbine-powered aircraft, a Vickers Viscount, departed Prestwick on 15 February 1953 for North America. It was followed by many more, as well as the BAC.111 twin-jet airliner and Hawker 125 business jet.

Under New Management

Together with Heathrow, Gatwick and Stansted on 1 April 1966, the British Airports Authority took over the facilities at Prestwick Airport from the Ministry of Aviation, including the air cargo and handling services, the airport still being designated the International Gateway to Scotland. In June 1971, Westburn House was taken over by BAA plc, as their engineering building. By this time, the area of the airport, with the addition of Runway 03/21, had grown to 1,299 acres and employed, with British Aerospace, some 1,500 persons.

The supersonic Concorde, 002, gave a flyby to 13,000 people at the airport on 28 June 1971 and on 1 July Prestwick was a refuelling stop on a transatlantic air race, where twenty-three general aviation aircraft were hosted by ATC and airport staff. The re-surfacing and strengthening of Runway 13/31 at Prestwick, with the addition of centre-line lighting, to accept all types of 'Jumbo' military, civil passenger and cargo transports, was completed in August 1971.

Five Westland Sea Kings of No.819 Squadron, RN, arrived on 27 October 1971, to provide anti-submarine defence and support for the British and

Resting in front of the terminal building, after their transatlantic crossing from Canada, Howard DGA-15, CF-NTY (Race 40) and Beechcraft 17, CF-GWL (Race 12), were positioning for the England to Victoria Centennial Air Race in July 1971. (Peter Berry)

Handley Page Jetstream 200, G-AXFV, (Race 32), flown by Captain Bill Bright, in the Victoria Centennial Air Race, spent just 11 minutes refuelling and completing formalities at Prestwick in July 1971. (Peter Berry)

US Navy Polaris submarine fleets in the Clyde Estuary. They also added a Search and Rescue role for both military and civil incidents. From 1972, RAF personnel from the Scottish Military Area Control Centre were also housed within the complex.

The Prestwick Flying Group was formed in October 1972, by a number of ATC, airport, business and SAL pilots. The chairman was Dr W.G. Watson, Scottish Aviation; vice-chairman Jack Newbery, BAA plc, Prestwick; Bill Pavitt, senior tower controller; chief pilot, Hugh Copland, airways controller and secretary, Peter Berry, oceanic controller. The first aircraft to be delivered on 24 February 1973 was a Piper Cherokee 180, G-AZSG. Both the Prestwick Flying Club and Flight Centre continue today. In October, a large area was opened at the airport for the handling of live animals arriving at the airport.

Although refuelled in just 10 minutes at Prestwick, during the 1971 Victoria Cenntenial Air Race, this Bellanca Viking, N8792V (Race 2), was forced to ditch into the Atlantic, after running out of fuel, south of Greenland. The crew were rescued. (Peter Berry)

Westland Sea King HAS.2A and HAS.5, helicopters of No.819 Squadron, Royal Navy arrived at Prestwick in 1971 and for thirty years, provided anti-submarine protection for the British and American nuclear deterrent in the Clyde. They also provided an important Air Sea Rescue role and XV674 pictured here, shows off its equipment at a 'Fly In' in 1976. (Peter Berry)

Commemorating the Orangefield Hotel and terminal building and the many services it provided during its long life, a large commemorative plaque of the airport was unveiled by the Duke of Hamilton in the departure lounge of the terminal at Prestwick on 25 January 1973. The Aviation murals which once graced the Orangefield Terminal walls are now preserved in a nearby indoor bowling green. The maple floor from the terminal dining room was re-laid in the conference room in the new terminal building. Adamton House was purchased by the Historic Productions Group and offered medieval-type banquets for their guests, and was later to accommodate students from the BAE Flying College at Prestwick. The house has now been restored as a hotel.

At the end of their service lives, a number of de Havilland Trident 1C airliners were flown to Prestwick in April 1974 and stored. The following year seven of these were cut up for scrap.

Above: The first aircraft to be delivered to the Prestwick Flying Group in 1973 was a 4-seat Piper Cherokee 180G, G-AZSG. It was used for air touring, as well as flying training. (Peter Berry)

Left: A large plaque of the airport was unveiled by the Duke of Hamilton in the International Departure Lounge at Prestwick on 25 January,1973. It commemorates the Orangefield Hotel and terminal building and the many services it provided during its long life. (Peter Berry)

New Instrument Landing System

In 1975, an updated Instrument Landing System (ILS) was installed at both ends of Runway 13/31 and new approach and runway lighting was installed. October saw at total of 101 passenger aircraft diverted to Prestwick, due to bad weather at their destinations.

British Caledonian Airways announced, in January 1978, their intention to site an £8 million Caledonian Airmotive engine overhaul facility on the Shawfarm Estate to the south of the airport, for the overhaul of the General Electric CF-6 turbofan engines, from their fleet of Douglas DC-10 transports. Opened in 1980, an increasing number of CF-6 engines continue to be overhauled by GE/Caledonian, for operators of Boeing 747, Airbus and Douglas DC-10 transports.

In service with BEA and British Airways for eleven years, six of the early DH.121 Trident Fleet, including G-ARPJ, were withdrawn from service and broken up at Prestwick in May 1976. (Cyril Lofthouse)

In 1980, British Caledonian Airways opened a facility on the Shawfarm Estate at Prestwick Airport to overhaul the General Electric CF6 engines from their fleet of Douglas DC-10 transports. GE/Caledonian continues to overhaul this engine today, from the many operators flying Boeing 747, Airbus and DC-10 transports. (Peter Berry)

Runway 03/21 Closed

To save rating expenditure of £800,000/year Runway 03/21 was closed in 1985, but with the commencement of flying training by the new British Aerospace Flying Training College in 1988, a short length was later re-opened.

Airport Golden Jubilee

In August 1985, Prestwick Airport celebrated its Golden Jubilee. Scottish Airports published a book ontaining contributions from many interested parties, relating to the highlights in the history of Scottish Aviation and the airport.

Prestwick Gateway Status

In May 1989, the charter airline, Air 2000, challenged the role of Prestwick as the Scottish Gateway Airport. Following a review of the operations at the Scottish Lowland Airports (Prestwick, Abbotsinch and Edinburgh) on 6 May 1990, exclusive transatlantic Gateway status was removed from Prestwick Airport. Air Canada cargo remained at Prestwick for the time being. The reduction of business at the airport also resulted in the closing of the airport shop and post office, the bank having closed some years previously. The first three months of 1990 saw that only 6,900 passengers had been handled as well as 4,729 tonnes of cargo.

The Atlantic Ferry Remembered

To celebrate the fiftieth anniversary of the Atlantic Air Ferry, many ageing pilots, servicing and repair ground crew, controllers and workers from many other trades, assembled in 1990 to remember that more than 20,000 military aircraft were delivered through Prestwick during the Second World War. Scottish Aviation Ltd (SAL) was warmly remembered as 'Safe at Last'. After servicing or modification at Prestwick, men and women pilots from the Air Transport Auxiliary (ATA) would then fly the various types of single, twin and four-engine aircraft to the RAF. In addition, some 15,000 transport, medical and weather flights crossed the North Atlantic to and from Prestwick.

Prestwick Airport Purchased

To safeguard their flying operations, from 1 April 1992 the airport was purchased from BAA by British Aerospace plc. Local interests formed PIK Ltd and acquired

To commemorate the fiftieth anniversary of the first arrival of a North Atlantic Ferry Flight at Prestwick on 29 November 1940, 'Safe at Last'. Many people who took part, from SAL, the ATA, TAC, RAF Transport Command, BOAC and ATFERO, gathered at the airport to remember the 37,000 flights completed during the war. (From a painting by Dugald Cameron, OBE)

the terminal building, the runway and taxi-way being retained by British Aerospace and then leased by PIK with much of the infrastructure. Only 11,000 passengers used the terminal in 1992/93 and air cargo totalled 16,000 tonnes. PIK began operations with just fifty-one employees. A hard period of returning the airport to a working, profitable operation was begun, with every aspect of the airport operation being examined and plans were laid for the rebuilding of the airport facilities and services.

The retention of Air Cargo was an important first step and in June Federal Express acquired a 10 per cent stake in PIK and signed a ten-year lease for their cargo facility. Runway 03/21 had its 6,000ft reinstated for crosswind landings, with a new surface, approach and runway lighting. An extension was also planned for all-weather landings by cargo-carrying B747s.

On 1 February 1993, PIK took over the handling of all aircraft from the apron services provided by Ogden Aviation and from 1 April PIK replaced the staff at the Civil Aviation Authority-operated control tower, with their own air traffic controllers and support staff. To attract more passengers to the airport, PIK applied for planning approval to construct a railway station on the Stranraer-Ayr-Glasgow railway line, with a covered air-bridge to the airport. This was a very similar facility to that shown on the terminal building drawings in 1960 and 1963. This work began on 29 November 1993.

Ryanair passenger services to and from Dublin opened in May 1994 and the spectator terrace was re-opened in June. The railway station, with its covered air-bridge to the terminal building, was opened on 5 September 1994. Free train connections between any manned station in Scotland and Prestwick Airport were offered to departing passengers. Arriving passengers were charged just £5 for the journey to any station in Scotland. An additional 1,000-space car park was opened, adjacent to the train station and at the end of the financial year in March 1995,

Looking north-east across Prestwick's long runway, the terminal area and railway station is to the left and the BAE SYSTEMS Structures and Regional Aircraft buildings are on the right. (PIK)

137,787 passengers had used the terminal and 26,000 tonnes of cargo were handled. From August, in a bid to hold operating costs, the airport was closed from 11.00 p.m. to 7.00 a.m. daily, due to no contracted air traffic. By March 1996, a total of 340,000 passengers used the terminal and air cargo totalled 39,500 tonnes.

Glasgow/Prestwick International

To add a further commercial signature to the west of Scotland airports, the designation Glasgow/Abbotsinch and Glasgow/Prestwick Airports was announced. A tall sculpture, 'Celestial Navigator', was erected at the entrance to Prestwick Airport. The year 1996/97 saw more than 542,000 passengers use the terminal building, and air cargo totalled 36,000 tonnes.

New Cargo Terminal

On Monday 15 December 1997 ground was broken at Prestwick, on the site of a new £8 million project for a new cargo terminal, completed in 1999. Located south of the parallel taxi-track, the facility offered nose-in parking for the range of large turbo-jet transport aircraft. Fifty wide-bodied cargo flights were being handled each week and a four-fold increase in cargo traffic was expected by the year 2002. A new cargo village was completed, providing 145,000sq. ft of capacity. This facility was opened on 22 December 1998. Instant nationwide trans-shipment direct from cargo-plane to vehicle truck commenced, with Debsmith European Transport, Concorde Express, Plane Trucking, Sutherlands and Ron Smith Transport.

In March 1998, Prestwick Airport returned to 24-hour operations. From 30 April, Stagecoach Bus acquired a 75 per cent holding in the airport for £41 million. The balance of 25 per cent was held by the executive chairman, Matthew Hudson. The new division, Stagecoach Aviation, operated the airport and related business. Glasgow/Prestwick Airport ended the financial year in March 1998, with a turnover of £21.7 million, making a £2.2 million profit and employing 385 people. In May, Runway 03/21 was resurfaced, with new approach and runway lighting. On 17 June, a new passenger arrivals hall was opened in the terminal building. Polar Air Cargo and its associates began assessing Prestwick as a maintenance base for their fleet of B747s, leading to a large 61,000sq. ft hangar, completed in June 2000.

A new 145,008 sq. ft air cargo terminal and village were completed at Prestwick in 1999, to handle the growing number of Boeing 747 freighter aircraft scheduled through the airport each week. Adjacent to the Terminal Apron, the facility offered nose-in parking and a nationwide trans-shipment from 'plane to road vehicle' commenced. (Peter Berry)

A new 61,000 sq. ft hangar for the maintenance of the fleet of Polar and Atlas Air Boeing 747F cargo transports was opened at the airport in 2000. (Peter Berry)

Purchase By INFRATIL

On 22 January 2001, INFRATIL, a New Zealand company, announced they had become the major shareholder in a consortium that had acquired the airport from Stagecoach. Almost 1 million passengers had used the terminal building during the previous twelve months, with 41,000 tonnes of air cargo being handled at the Air Cargo Centre. By 31 April, airport revenue totalled £25 million, 55 per cent from passengers, 30 per cent from air cargo and 15 per cent from General Aviation, Property and Maintenance.

Prestwick's long and wide Runway 13/31, the longest civil runway in Scotland, continues to attract the largest civil and military aircraft. The Prestwick Flight Centre moved into new premises alongside the control tower during 2004, together with an adjacent hangar for aircraft maintenance. Flying training, touring and parking for private aircraft are offered.

With the decommissioning of No.819 Squadron, RN, in November 2002, three Sea Kings remained, becoming the SAR Flight, HMS *Gannet*, and providing search and rescue services within some 200 nautical miles of Prestwick. Response times are 15 minutes during the day and 45 minutes at night, 24 hours a day. A total of 243 'scrambles' were completed in 2003.

The Prestwick Airport Aviation Group (PAAG) celebrated their fiftieth anniversary in 2003 and the protection of Controlled Airspace was returned to Prestwick Airport on 30 October. Construction also began of the Ryanair Service hangar for their fleet of 189-seat, Boeing 737-800 series aircraft, which was opened in May 2004. The 120,000sq. ft Goodrich Aircraft Service Centre building on the new Aerospace Park site, just north of the airport boundary, was opened in the summer and a new 20,000sq. ft maintenance, repair and overhaul building is planned. A total of 1.97 million passengers used the terminal building for the twelve months to March 2004. In August, INFRATL, in response to the increasing number of passengers using the airport, announced a £3 million package of improvements to passenger check-in facilities, with more retail outlets.

Now moved into new quarters, with the adjacent maintenance hangar, the Prestwick Flight Centre continues to maintain the long history of flying training at Prestwick. (Peter Berry)

Pictured here in October 2004, is one of three Westland Sea King HU.5 SAR helicopters, XZ578, PW708, operated by the SAR Flight at HMS *Gannet*, Prestwick. The crew are boarding to exercise with a Royal Navy ship in the Firth of Clyde. Out of service Ryanair B737-200 and Prestwick Airport's B747, N852FT, are shown behind. (Peter Berry)

To maintain their fleet of 189-seat Boeing 737-800 aircraft, Ryanair opened a hangar and maintenance facility at Prestwick in 2004, alongside the Polar Air Cargo hangar. (Peter Berry)

Completed in 2004, the 120,000 sq. ft Goodrich Service Centre in the Aerospace Park, adjacent to Prestwick Airport, overhauls a large range of aircraft engine and ancillary systems. (Peter Berry)

Shown in 2004, the Glasgow/Prestwick Terminal now boasts a railway station on the Stranraer-Ayr-Glasgow railway line, as well as Stagecoach Express coaches to Glasgow and a new M77 Motorway from Glasgow to the Airport. (Peter Berry)

A modern and vibrant image, underlined by the Glaswegian slogan 'Pure Dead Brilliant' was featured in the re-furbished Terminal Building, launched at Glasgow/Prestwick Airport on 19 May 2005. (Peter Berry)

Prestwick Airport from the air in October 2004 showing the consolidation of services around the airport, including the Ryanair and Polar hangars, centre left and Goodrich Service Centre, top right. (Prestwick Flight Centre)

Chapter Four

Passenger and Air-Cargo Services, 1945–2004

The sudden ending of the war with Japan in August 1945 released some twenty Douglas C-54/DC-4 transports to PanAmerican Airlines, TWA and American Overseas Airlines (AOA) for an early start to commercial transatlantic services. At this time, British transatlantic services were flown by three Boeing flying-boats from Foynes, on the River Shannon, and the twelve Liberators of the Return Ferry Service at Prestwick. As a sign for the future, an AOA DC-4 (NX90901) landed at Prestwick on a proving flight on 22 September 1945, followed by another AOA DC-4 (NC90902) in October.

Following the end of the Second World War, the American Overseas Airline was to make commercial proving flights to Europe. Douglas DC-4, 'Flagship New York', N90902, is shown at Prestwick in October 1945. (BAE SYSTEMS)

Immediately after the war, Flugfelag Islands (Icelandic Airways) opened a trial service from Reykjavik to Largs, using a Consolidated Catalina, TF-ISP. The first arrival was in July 1945 and in September the service continued to Copenhagen. From May 1946, 14-seat Liberators were leased from Scottish Airlines and used as far as Prestwick and then DC-3s on to Copenhagen. This service closed in April 1948, when Flugfelag DC-4s entered service.

Scottish Airlines

Scottish Airlines was formed on 1 January 1946 and from 28 January began a return Prestwick to Belfast/Sydenham service with a 21-seat DC-3, G-AGWS. The fare was 30 shillings, single (£1.50). From 16 September the evening flights

Shown in front of the Orangefield Terminal in 1946, Douglas DC-3, G-AGWS, served with Scottish Airlines on domestic routes. Marked WZ984, it was later flown on military troop contracts during 1951/52, until disposed of to Canada. (via Dougal McIntyre)

The Fokker F.XXII, G-AFZP, was used by Scottish Airlines after the war for a few passenger flights on the Belfast service, but then continued with pleasure flights from Prestwick until it retired in 1947. (E.J. Riding)

1. Pictured on the apron at Prestwick, a colourful Lockheed C-130E Hercules, AF63-7899, was flown by the USAF Military Airlift Command. (Jim Cain)

2. Seen on take-off from Runway 31 at Prestwick in 2004, Short Belfast, G-HLFT, served with the RAF as XR365. This one and a sister ship are believed to be the only ones flying. (Jim Cain)

3. *Above:* The base aircraft for the USAF, Military Air Transport Service at Prestwick, from August 1952 to 1965 was Douglas VC-47D, AF45-1057. (Jim Cain)

4. *Below:* Shown using most of Prestwick's 9,800ft of Runway 31, Antonov 124, RA-82080, of Polet Cargo Airlines, departs on 20 September 2004 with a 45-tonne load of cargo for Ontario, California. (Fred Seggie)

5. Pictured during the summer of 2004, SAL Twin Pioneer, G-APRS, is the only airworthy example in the UK. Registered to Scottish Aviation in January 1959, she served with several operators, before becoming XT610, '22', with the Empire Test Pilots School in 1965. Today, she flies as *Primrose*, with Air Atlantique. (Andrew McClymont)

6. En route to the National Aviation Museum in Ottawa, Canada, in 1968, Consolidated B-24L Liberator Mk.VIII, marked HE773, had been acquired from the Indian Air Force. Earlier it had served with the RAF as KN820. (Peter Berry)

7. Shown departing Prestwick for New York in May 1970, BOAC Vickers Super VC-10, G-ASGP, joined the RAF in 1981 as a military transport, marked ZD242, and was later converted to a VC-10, K.4. tanker. (Peter Berry)

8. At Bay 4 at Prestwick in February 1970, Bristol Freighter 31, CF-YDO, was on its delivery flight to Lamb Airways in Canada. (Peter Berry)

9. *Above:* Marked 'Arctic Seven', Canadian Douglas DC-3, CF-CSC, in transit through Prestwick in 1971, was owned by D.G. Harris Productions. (Peter Berry)

10. *Below:* Seen in front of the Westburn House at Prestwick in June 1973, Vickers Viscount 700, G-AMON, named *Scottish Princess*, was leased from Cambrian Airways by BOAC to feed the transatlantic services to North America. (Gordon Macadie)

11. Parked in front of Westburn House at Prestwick in May 1973, Canadair T-33AN Silver Star, N12420, had served with the military as CAF.21200 and was in transit from Chico, USA, to Turin in Italy for a cloud-seeding contract. Upon arrival it was marked I-NUBY. (Gordon Macadie)

12. Douglas DC-6B, OO-VGK, was one of sixty-eight charter flights which brought 11,000 French and German football supporters into Prestwick in May 1976 for the European Cup Final between Bayern Munich and St Etienne at Hampden Park, Glasgow. (Gordon Macadie)

13. Lockheed 1011-100 Tristar, G-BDCW, Fleet Number '101', is shown diverted to Prestwick in April 1976. It was delivered to Gulf Air for passenger services from the Middle East to London. (Peter Berry)

14. DH.98 Mosquito B.35, G-MOSI/RS709 appeared in the film *633 Squadron*. Shown here at Prestwick in July 1984, she was being flown by retired test pilot, George Aird, to the USAF Museum at Dayton, Ohio. (Peter Berry)

15. *Above:* Lockheed RP-3D Orion, Bu.158227, from the US Naval Oceanographic Office, visited Prestwick in August 1989. It was engaged in 'Project Magnet', the surveying of the Earth's magnetic field. (Peter Berry)

16. *Below:* Pictured here at Prestwick is the Military Air Transport Service Lockheed C-121A Constellation, N494TW, en route to the Farnborough Air Show in 1998. As AF48-609, she was a frequent visitor to Prestwick during the Cold War years and served on the Berlin Airlift. (Peter Berry)

terminated at Aldergrove, as there was no night flying equipment at Sydenham. The remaining Fokker F.XXII, G-AFZP, made one or two trips on the Belfast service and was then fitted with 525hp P&W Wasp engines and used for local joy-rides from Prestwick. It was withdrawn from service in August 1947 and became a hangar queen, until it was broken up in July 1952. A summer service in 1946 with DC-3s linked Prestwick and Copenhagen with the Faroe Islands.

The BOAC Return Ferry Service, routeing Prestwick to Montreal, suffered a loss on 21 February 1946, when Liberator AL528, Captain E. Poole, made a forced landing at Charlotte, Prince Edward Island, the co-pilot being killed, but three crew and eight passengers escaped. By November 1946, the BOAC Return Ferry Service had completed 2,392 crossings of the North Atlantic from Prestwick, carrying some 22,500 passengers, 3.5 million pounds of mail and urgent war supplies.

Scheduled transatlantic commercial flights began through Prestwick on 21 May 1946, when a KLM DC-4 PH-TAR arrived from Amsterdam en route to New York. This was followed on 16 September when the Scandinavian Airline System (SAS) DC-4, SE-BBC arrived at Prestwick from Stavanger and Copenhagen, en route to New York. Several other transatlantic airliners appeared on the Orangefield apron, having been diverted to Prestwick due weather at their destination.

Scottish Aviation converted a number of Liberators to 24/30-seat transports and in March 1946 a transatlantic survey flight was made to San Diego, California. These flights led to the airline gaining charters with their Liberators to North America, the Middle East and within Europe. From July 1946 Scottish Airlines began a service from Prestwick to Amsterdam for Royal Dutch Airlines (KLM) using DC-3s. Scottish Airlines, under contract to Iceland Airways, from 16 September linked Iceland with New York, via Gander, using Liberators. From 20 September, Scottish Airlines flew a Prestwick to Paris service via Manchester, under contract to Air France, using DC-3s. In their first year of operation Scottish Airlines carried 2,912 passengers, 16,000lb of cargo and 26,500lb of mail.

An early Scandinavian Airline System arrival at Prestwick on 16 September 1946, was this Douglas DC-4, SE-BBC, *Passad*. It was operating the first Stavanger and Copenhagen service to New York, via Prestwick and Gander. (via Alisdair Cochrane)

Pictured arriving at Prestwick on 1 March 1946, this TWA Lockheed L-049 Constellation, diverted from Paris due to bad weather, was one of the early conversions from the military C-69 transports. (Scottish Aviation)

Lockheed L-049 Constellation PP-PCF, of Panair do Brazil, named *Manoel de Borba Gato*, was the first scheduled foreign arrival at London, Heathrow, from Buenos Aires, but it is shown here at Prestwick on 16 April 1946. (Scottish Aviation)

Delivered from Gander to Prestwick on 23 October 1941, Consolidated B-24C, Liberator II, AL552, served with the RAF as G-AHZR, Scottish Airlines received the CofA on 3 December 1946 and it is pictured over Prestwick in 1947. Two years later, it was flown by Hellenic Airlines as SX-DAB and then by STAAP as F-BEDS. (via Gordon Macadie)

Founder David McIntyre was keen to begin a transatlantic passenger service to New York. Scottish Airlines Consolidated Liberator II, G-AGZH/AL571, flown by Captain John Dobson, was loaded with cargo and departed from Prestwick on 16 March, 1946, for the survey flight. The proposed single fare was £80. (via Dougal McIntyre)

Nationalisation of Air Services

The Nationalisation of British scheduled air services on 1 August 1946 saw Scottish Airlines flying return services under contract to BEA, with DC-3s from Prestwick to London, via Renfrew, Prestwick to London, London to Aberdeen, via Edinburgh and Renfrew to Belfast. From March 1947, Air France operated a three-times-weekly service from Prestwick to Paris, first with DC-3s and later with Sud Est Lanquedoc transports. Scottish Air Express, a Division of SAL, marketed Inclusive Tours from Prestwick to several destinations in Europe at affordable fares.

The wartime service from Montreal to Prestwick, operated for the Canadian Government by Trans-Canada Air Lines, continued in their own name from 9 July 1946, still using Avro Lancastrians. The route was extended to London on 15 September. From 11 September 1946 the Wednesday BOAC Constellation service from London to New York was routed via Prestwick and Gander. The first non-stop New York to Prestwick flight was made on 6 December by the BOAC Constellation G-AHEM, *Balmoral*, in 11 hours 2 minutes. Several medical flights have also been reported by BOAC, between Prestwick and Switzerland, with patients who had contracted Tuberculosis.

Trans-Canada Air Lines replaced their ageing Lancastrians with Canadair DC-4M *North Stars* on their service from Montreal to London, via Prestwick on 15/16 April 1947, carrying eighteen passengers. KLM replaced Scottish Airlines on the Prestwick to Amsterdam route in April, extending the route to New York in May. From 6 October, they introduced the L-749 Constellation. Scottish Airlines continued to offer charter services from Prestwick and American Overseas Airlines (AOA) commenced a twice-weekly service through Prestwick on 1 June from New York and Reykjavik to Oslo/Stockholm and Helsinki with DC-4s, soon replacing them with Constellations. On 3 September, AOA had logged 15,000 crossings of the North Atlantic, including their flights during the war years.

Replacing the Trans-Canada Air Line Lancastrians in April 1947, Canadair DC-4M2, North Star, CF-TFE, boards passengers at Prestwick for the flight to Montreal. (via Gordon Macadie)

In June 1947 the Scottish Airline fleet included the five Liberators, thirteen DC-3s and one Fokker F.XXII. For local joy-riding an Airspeed Oxford, G-AHDZ, was flown for several years, joined by two Percival Proctor aircraft, G-AHMP and HMT. Two Supermarine Walrus amphibians were prepared by Scottish Aviation, G-AJNO for Scottish Airlines, for a service to Brodick Bay on the Isle of Arran and HFN, from the whaling company of Charles Mauritzen. In the event, JNO did not enter service and HFN foundered in gales at Loch Ryan, Stranraer, on 3 July 1955. The services for BEA terminated in July 1947, but a Belgian airline, COBETA, with Scottish Aviation interests, opened a twice-weekly service from Brussels to Prestwick via Manchester in July, using DC-3s. A service was also flown from Brussels to Lydda.

From August 1947, five of Scottish Airline's Dakotas joined other British airlines in Operation Pakistan, providing an airlift to some 8,500 refugees from India to Pakistan after the division at Indian Independence. This was followed in October by six DC-3s evacuating Indians from Pakistan. By the year end, Scottish Airlines had a fleet of twenty aircraft, eighty-five aircrew and had carried 43,702 passengers, 163,500lb cargo and 36,000lb of mail. But charters were slowly reducing and Scottish Airlines turned to assist the start-up of Luxembourg Airlines, providing DC-3s for their services to Frankfurt, Paris, Zurich and Lydda. They also took a 40 per cent interest in Hellenic Airlines and from March 1948 began a twice-weekly service from London to Cairo, via Paris, Rome and Athens, using Liberators. Services with DC-4s and DC-3s were also begun from Athens to Cyprus, Alexandria, Port Said and Lydda.

Pictured outside the hangar at Prestwick, the re-furbished Supermarine Walrus, G-AJNO, is resplendent in Scottish Airlines colours. Intended for a service to Brodick Bay, Isle of Arran, she did not enter service. Her sister, JNP, intended for whale-spotting in the Antarctic, foundered en-route to Stranraer. (via Dougal McIntyre)

Scottish Aviation converted RAF Douglas Dakota III, FL518, to G-AJLZ. From February 1948, as LX-LAA, it was operated by Luxembourg Airlines on routes to Frankfurt, Paris and Zurich. (via Alisdair Cochrane)

Following service with the Scottish Airlines as G-AGZI, this consolidated Liberator II was flown from February 1948, by Hellenic Airlines, SX-DAA, named *Maid of Athens*. (via Dougal Mcintyre)

Shown on the Orangefield Apron in September 1950, Hellenic Airlines Douglas DC-4, SX-DAC, named *Hellas*, linked Greece with Cyprus, Egypt and Israel. (via Gordon Macadie)

Berlin Airlift

On 11 June 1948 the Russians mounted a surface blockade of the routes into Berlin. The Allied response was to organise a Military/Civil Airlift, which maintained the City until the ground routes were re-opened on 12 May 1949. Scottish Airlines joined Operation Plainfare with two DC-3 and three Liberator aircraft. Their contribution totalled:

		Freighter Sorties	Tons	Tanker Sorties	Tons
Dakota	G-AGWS	51	175.9		
Dakota	G-AGZF	50	172.2		
Liberator	G-AHDY			233	1,534.0
Liberator	G-AHZP	15	110.1		
Liberator	G-AHZR			148	1,182.5
Totals		116	458.2	381	2,716.5

Scottish Airlines were charted by the Milk Marketing Board from August through October 1948 to fly milk from Belfast to Liverpool. One Liberator was lost, landing at Liverpool.

Prestwick suffered their first major civil transport accident on 21 October 1948. A KLM Lockheed Constellation, PH-TEN, *Nijmegen* completed a GCA approach to Runway 31, but overshot, due to crosswinds and circled at 700ft for a visual approach, landing into wind on Runway 26. While positioning for landing, the flight ran into cloud and collided with electric pylon cables near Tarbolton, ENE of Prestwick. Captain K.D. Parmentier and thirty-nine passengers and crew were killed.

AOA introduced the L-049 Constellation on the Prestwick service from 30 November 1948 and an Icelandic Airways DC-4 service from Reykjavik to London via Prestwick was begun in 1949. During the year KLM operated the first weekly all-cargo service through Prestwick to New York. The scheduled service by Scottish Airlines, Prestwick to the Isle of Man continued with Rapides or DC-3s. Their aircraft fleet at November 1949 had reduced to five DC-3s, four Liberators and a Rapide.

Liberator AL522 had served with the BOAC RFS since 1944 and continued in service as G-AHYD after the war. It was then modified by Scottish Aviation and between February and May 1948 a flight-refuelling trial took place over the North Atlantic, Lancastrian tankers from Shannon and Goose Bay, delivering 600 gallons of fuel in just 10 minutes. A total of fifty-six flights were completed, but this was the last civil application of the technique. The last of 3,000 transatlantic crossings by BOAC Return Ferry Service Liberators between Prestwick and Montreal was completed at the end of September 1949, when the Liberators were withdrawn from service. Since September 1946, only cargo and mail had been carried and

Above: Delivered from Gander to Prestwick on 13 December 1941, Consolidated B-24C, Liberator II, AL522, served with the RAF until it was converted by Scottish Aviation in July 1944, for the BOAC Return Ferry Service. Registered G-AHYD in 1946 it continued in service, until modified by Scottish Aviation for flight refuelling trials which took place over the North Atlantic in February 1948. The re-fuelling receptacle can been seen, underneath the tail. (Peter M. Bowers)

Opposite top: The first Boeing 377 Stratocruiser to be delivered to BOAC, G-AKGH, is shown here at Prestwick, with appropriate accompaniment, on 1 July 1950, where she was named 'RMA Caledonia'. (BOAC 5882)

Opposite middle: American Overseas Airlines placed Boeing Stratocruisers on their New York–Prestwick–Amsterdam–Frankfurt route in January 1950. Shown here is N90941, named *Flagship Great Britain.* (AOA)

Opposite bottom: Pictured in front of the Orangefield Terminal on August 28 1951, the mighty 100-seat, Bristol Brabazon, G-AGPW, was first flown on 4 September 1949. Found to be too large and too expensive to operate, the sole prototype was scrapped in October 1953. (via Gordon Macadie)

from 1 April 1949, this service continued three-times weekly, with Scottish Airlines providing the crews.

Following the re surfacing of the runways at Prestwick in 1949, the BOAC service from London–New York service, via Prestwick, was flown by Boeing Stratocruisers from 6 December and from 10 January 1950 AOA replaced its Lockheed Constellations with Stratocruisers on the New York–Prestwick–Amsterdam–Frankfurt route. From May, KLM introduced Constellations with thirty sleeping-berths on their route Amsterdam–Prestwick–New York. By the summer, weekly scheduled services through Prestwick totalled seventy-nine and were noted as, KLM–27, SAS–20, BOAC–12, TCA–7, AOA–7, Air France–3 and Scottish Airlines–3. PanAm opened an office at Prestwick and the AOA routes were taken over by PanAm on 25 October 1950.

As a BEA Associate, Scottish Airlines flew DC-3 services on a Prestwick–Burtonwood–Northolt route from May 1951 to February 1953, and in 1951 KLM introduced on 26 May a Constellation sleeper service from Amsterdam to New York, via Prestwick. The first visit by a Comet jet-airliner occurred on 5 April 1951 and a visit by the mighty Brabazon transport attracted 3,000 spectators on 28 August.

PanAm operated their first DC-6B service through Prestwick, introducing 'tourist-class' fares on 7 June 1952, and on 7 August a DH Comet from

AKGH

AMERICAN OVERSEAS AIRLINES

Johannesburg was diverted from London due to poor weather. A BOAC B377 Stratocruiser, G-AKGL, was damaged landing at Prestwick on 25 April 1951, when the nose-wheel was broken. It was repaired at Prestwick.

Following re-structuring, a new company, Scottish Airlines (Prestwick), was registered on 28 September 1951 and continued limited scheduled and charter services from Prestwick. In September, Scottish Airlines bought three Avro York transports to fulfil an Air Ministry Contract for flying military personnel to Montreal. These aircraft were converted at Prestwick, with fifty rear-facing seats, and was based at Stansted, entering service in early 1953. Scottish Airlines also used the Yorks during the summer of 1953 for air-cargo charters for Trans-Canada Air Lines from London to Montreal, via Prestwick. Overhauls at Stansted were completed in an ex-RAF hangar and during 1954 four more Yorks were acquired, with further contracts for trooping flights to Malta, Cyprus and the Middle East. These flights terminated in 1958. A total of five Yorks were lost in accidents and the two remaining ones were sold.

From February 1953, Scottish Airlines withdrew their Prestwick to London air service. From 7 October, a BOAC London to Trinidad service was opened with L-049 Constellations, via Prestwick, Gander, Bermuda and Barbados. TCA served London from Toronto, via Prestwick, from 1 November, with the pressurised Canadair DC-4M *North Star.* These transports were replaced by Lockheed L-1049C Super Constellations when, on 14 May 1954, TCA introduced an initial first/tourist-class service, with their Lockheed L-1049E Super Constellations from Montreal to London, via Prestwick. Later services were added, calling at Prestwick four times a week. In their later lives, the early marks of Super Constellations were upgraded with wing-tip fuel tanks to Lockheed L-1049G models.

BOAC suffered the loss of Stratocruiser, G-ALSA *Cathay*, Captain W.L. Stewart, on the morning of Christmas Day in 1954. Following a GCA approach to Runway 31 at Prestwick, the aircraft undershot the threshold and broke up on the runway. Twenty-eight people lost their lives; seven crew and one passenger survived.

From March 1955, Airwork Atlantic introduced a Douglas DC-4s and later Douglas DC-6A, on a twice-weekly all-cargo service from London to New York, via Manchester, Prestwick, Keflavik, Gander and Montreal. The service was suspended on 18 December. During the year, BOAC leased three Lockheed L-1049D Super Constellations to upgrade their Coronet tourist service from London to New York, via Prestwick. On a lighter note, 'Woody' Woods, the pilot of the Cumberland Air Taxi, D.H. Dragon Rapide G-ALPK, flew into Prestwick during the summer of 1959 for pleasure flying and *ad hoc* charters.

To cope with the increasing number of British emigrants wishing to settle in Canada, the Canadian Government chartered a number of DC-4M and Super Constellation transports from TCA, as well as DC-6Bs from Canadian Pacific. These charters were extended to DC-4s from Maritime Central and Wheeler Airlines.

Following the uprising in Hungary in 1956, a large number of refugees also wished to settle in Canada. Even more capacity was now required and Flying

Thirty-two members of the retail household furniture store, A. Cochrane & Sons, Newmilns Ltd, were treated in August 1952 to a Scottish Airlines charter flight from Prestwick to Belfast, in this Douglas DC-3. (Ronnie Jay)

Trans-Canada Air Lines introduced the Lockheed L-1049E Super Constellation into service, via Prestwick on 14 May 1954. With the addition of tip-tanks, CF-TGF, '406', now a L-1049G, is shown here, back-tracking Runway 31 for take-off. (Gordon Macadie)

Seen loading at London, Heathrow, the BOAC Boeing Stratocruiser G-ALSA, *Cathay*, was later lost at Prestwick early in the morning on Christmas Day 1954, when she undershot landing on Runway 31 at Prestwick and broke up, with the loss of twenty-eight passengers and crew. (BOAC 5828)

Nestled among the cocooned Canadair Sabre jets at Prestwick in summer 1959, 'Woody' Wood's DH.89 Dragon Rapide, G-ALPK, takes a break from joy-riding and the odd charter flight. (Gordon Macadie)

Tiger, Slick and Great Lakes Airlines joined this 'Air Bridge' from London and Prestwick to Canada with their DC-4 transports. By the end of 1957, some 17,656 emigrants and refugees had been flown to Canada in 207 flights.

By June 1957, additional DC-4 capacity was sought from General Airways, Meteor Air Transport, Californian Eastern Aviation and Overseas National Airways. SABENA also joined the 'non-scheduled' carriers with their Douglas DC-7Cs. Flights were routed from Vienna and Heathrow and via Prestwick or Shannon en route to Edmonton, Moncton, Montreal, Toronto, Vancouver and Winnipeg. The first departures from Heathrow were on 24 November 1956, by a Maritime Central DC-4 and a Canadian Pacific DC-6B. Flights via Prestwick commenced on 15 March 1957, with the DC-4s of Great Lakes, Flying Tiger and Slick. Using the last of their long-range DC-7C transports, KLM began service from Amsterdam to New York, via Prestwick, on 3 June.

Signalling the end of the long-range propeller era, the Bristol Britannia turbo-prop began a BOAC London to Chicago service, via Prestwick, Montreal and Detroit on 6 May 1958. By the end of the year, Scottish Airlines had just one 36-seat DC-3 G-AMPP left from its fleet of transport aircraft and continued the scheduled service from Prestwick to the Isle of Man. Early in 1961, the Dakota and scheduled air service were sold to Dan-Air and Scottish Airlines withdrew from the airline scene.

Turbo-Jet Services

Following the opening of the lengthened Runway 13/31 to 9,800ft in 1960, turbo-jet services began at Prestwick on 27 May, with a BOAC Boeing707, G-APFB, routeing from London to New York. From 1 June, Air Canada introduced the Douglas DC-8-41 on the Montreal to London route; PanAm, KLM, SAS and Seaboard & Western all brought their DC-8/B707 fleets into service through Prestwick. Both BOAC and PanAm flew all-cargo piston-engine, Douglas DC-7F transports from New York to London, via Prestwick, the first on 3 December.

Many colourful charter flights were using Prestwick in 1962: Capital, Riddle, SAS, Flying Tiger, Saturn, KLM, Aerlinte, Lufthansa, CPA, SABENA, Wardair, British Caledonian and Aeroflot. From 3 February, CSA leased a Britannia 318 from Cubana and routed their Prague to Havana service via Shannon/Prestwick and Gander.

PanAm operated their last DC-7C scheduled service on 27 September 1963, being replaced by a DC-8 via Keflavik. BOAC were reported to oppose the renewal of Fifth Freedom rights to SAS and KLM at Prestwick. This action later removed the airlines from landing at Prestwick. Trans-Canada continued their Montreal–Prestwick–London route, with Douglas DC-8-54CF transports.

Air-cargo services with PanAmerican Boeing 707s began in 1964 and, because of passenger demand, from August 1964 BOAC used the DH Comet 4 turbo-jet for service between Prestwick and New York, via Gander.

Shown taxying in at Prestwick in August 1969, BOAC Boeing 707-420, G-APFM, would shortly leave for the service to New York. (Peter Berry)

Pictured departing Runway 13 at Prestwick in August 1969 for Toronto, is Air Canada Douglas DC-8-41, CF-TJA. (Peter Berry)

PanAmerican Boeing 707-321C, N446PA, named *Clipper Climax*, prepares to depart for New York, from the apron at Prestwick in May 1970. (Peter Berry)

A Scandinavian Airlines DC-8-31, LN-MOA, named *Haakon Viking*, is shown departing Prestwick for North America in August 1968. (Peter Berry)

Pictured taxying in at Prestwick in August 1968, is Caledonian Airways Bristol Britannia, G-ATMA, named *County of Midlothian*. Inclusive Tour charters were operated from Prestwick to New York. (Peter Berry)

British Caledonian Airways received approval on 1 April 1965 for inclusive tours, with Britannias from London to New York, via Prestwick, and from August for a few weeks BOAC operated Comet services to Gander and Montreal. Emerald Airways began a service from Prestwick to Belfast, using DH Heron aircraft, replaced by Short SC-7 Skyvans and then DC-3s, the following year.

From 13 January 1966, BOAC began air-cargo services with B707-320C transports, from London to New York, via Manchester and Prestwick. BOAC also introduced, on 1April, the Vickers Super VC-10, G-ASGD, onto its London to Montreal and Chicago service, via Prestwick. In June 1966, Cammel Laird took over SAL and the USAF Air Rescue Squadron left Prestwick for Moron AFB in Spain. Air cargo tonnage through Prestwick had increased from 1,000 tonnes in 1951, to 10,000 tonnes by 1966.

KLM introduced a 1967 summer service from Prestwick to Amsterdam with DC-9s. On 21 June, Trans International operated their first DC-8-63 charter flight from Detroit, carrying 261 passengers. Members of the Prestwick Branch of Royal Air Force Association (RAFA), with colleagues from the Airport, ATC and HMS *Gannet*, staged the first bi-annual Prestwick Air Show on 30 September 1967. Emerald Airways ceased trading on 15 November.

From 22 May 1968, Ulster Air Transport resumed a service to Belfast. The KLM summer service was operated by Lockheed Electras and KLM transferred their air-cargo flight to Glasgow. In October, SAS ceased passenger service to Prestwick. In November, BEA began an intensive crew training programme with BAC.111-500 aircraft. Prestwick continued to attract a number of interesting aircraft in transit, a B-24 Liberator, with its 'shepherd' Canadair CL-28 Argus, a French Air Force Douglas C-47B and a Biafran aid Douglas DC-6B.

Parked at Bay 2, Prestwick, on 19 September 1969, this French Air Force Douglas C-47B, 14654, was severely damaged during a gale that very evening and was written off. (Peter Berry)

Six transport aircraft were refurbished by Scottish Aviation in 1969 for the Biafran Airlift to provide aid to the war-torn country. Douglas DC-6B, TF-AAF, at Prestwick, bears the title *Flughjalp*, 'Aid by Air'. (Gordon Macadie)

USAF MAC charters were noted in April 1969 by Capitol Airways, Trans Caribbean Airways, Overseas National Airways, Universal and TWA. Summer charters were flown by Martinair, Canadian Pacific, Donaldson International and American Flyers Airline. Spantax Convair 990s operated fortnightly inclusive tours to Palma. The last KLM DC-9 flight departed to Amsterdam. KLM operated their last DC-8 flight from New York to Amsterdam on 16 October. SAS began a twice-weekly air cargo service to Copenhagen, with DC-9s.

Prestwick's record of fog-free diversion status was put to the test in December 1969, when on 9 December sixteen international flights were diverted to the airport due to weather. Three days later a total of fifty-nine diversions were handled. The largest diversion day at Prestwick totalled eighty-eight jet and turbo-prop airliners diverted to the airport. One arriving flight, receiving landing clearance, was heard to say, 'Prestwick, Safe at Last'.

In January 1970, some 5,050 crew training movements by BEA, BOAC, Court Line, Dan-Air, Laker Airways and Monarch Airlines were recorded at Prestwick. In the summer, BOAC began a Vickers Super VC-10 service to Montreal and Chicago, via Prestwick. Also a once-weekly service to Boston and New York continued tours to Palma and SAM used Sud Est Caravelles for tours to Venice. Aeroflot offered the first tours to Leningrad. Aeroflot began several charters to Prestwick, using Ilyushin IL.62 and Tupolev Tu.104 transports.

Shown at Prestwick in May 1970, Ilyushin IL-62, CCCP-86676, was providing a charter flight from Moscow to the United States. (Peter Berry)

Flights between Prestwick and Moscow, were made with Tupolev Tu.104, CCCP-42448, during the summer of 1970. (Peter Berry)

The first visit by a Boeing 747 'Jumbo-jet' was a BOAC demonstration flight by G-AWNC on 1 August 1970. Two days later, a PanAm B747 PA120 diverted in to Prestwick with 333 passengers, due to fog at London/Heathrow. Laker gained Inclusive Tours from Prestwick to the US with B707s. BOAC, Air Canada, SAS and Seaboard World operated air-cargo services through Prestwick for an annual total of 20,000 tonnes/£97 million. The 1970s saw a feast of interesting aircraft types in transit through Prestwick, including Bristol 170, McKinnon Turbo Goose, Canadair CL-66B, Several Douglas DC-3s, a North American B-25 Mitchell, Douglas A-26 Marksman, a Consolidated Catalina, Hawker Sea Fury, Convair 880, Lockheed Tristar, Canadair T-33AN, Casa.352L, and CASA 2.111E.

The first USAF MATS, Lockheed C-5A Galaxy transport, AF69-0019, landed at Prestwick on 2 February 1972, diverted from Mildenhall due to bad weather. For the summer of 1972, BOAC introduced a Boeng 747 service from Manchester and Prestwick to New York. Seaboard World closed their Prestwick base in September. The last scheduled flight by SAS was with a Douglas DC-8, LN-MOC on 31 October 1972 and SAS transferred their air-cargo service to Glasgow.

On 7 April 1973, Laker Airways began the operation of Douglas DC-10 charter services from Prestwick to Toronto and from 1 June British Caledonian opened a daily London–Manchester–Prestwick scheduled service to New York. From 30 April, BAC Concorde G-BSST, was based at Prestwick for continuing test flights.

The fuel crisis in 1974 was to result in the cut-back of many charter services. The fuel crisis also affected PanAm services through Prestwick, which were terminated on 2 January, but cargo services continued with Boeing 747

An early B747 diversion to Prestwick on 2 May 1970, PanAmerican Boeing 747-121, N752PA, named *Clipper Fortune*, is shown here for engine repair. This 'Jumbo-jet' was soon to be destroyed by terrorists at Cairo Airport, Egypt, on 6 September 1970. (Peter Berry)

A frequent visitor to Prestwick in the early 1970s, a McKinnon turbo-prop conversion of the Grumman Goose, G-ASXG, was en-route to a fishing holiday in the Scottish Lochs. (Peter Berry)

An Allison-powered, turbo-prop Convairliner, was the prototype Canadair CL-66B. It is shown at Prestwick in June 1971, as a Canadian Armed Forces, CC-109, marked 109151. (Peter Berry)

Impounded at Prestwick in December 1973 for non-payment of fees, this North American B-25J Mitchell, with a film camera nose, had been used by Jeff Hawks for aerial photography. Later it was taken by road, to be displayed at the Imperial War Museum Collection at Duxford. (Cyril Lofthouse)

Refuelling at Prestwick on 13 August 1974, Douglas A-26B Invader, N60XY, had been converted to a Marksman Executive and was owned by the Oxxidental Oil Co. (Cyril Lofthouse)

Consolidated PBY-5A Catalina, N4760C, is shown at Prestwick in 1976, with its magnetic anomaly detector tail boom. It was operated by Terra Surveys/Geoterrex, during the search for gas and oil reserves around the coast of Scotland. Restored in 1992, it is on display at McChord AFB, Washington, as an OA-10A, marked 44-34033. (Peter Berry)

Hawker Sea Fury FB.11, CF-CHB, marked WH589, was part of the Ormond Haydon-Baillie Collection of military aircraft. It is seen in transit through Prestwick on 23 November 1973. (Peter Berry)

Owned by Rowandrill Inc. and flown by Bob Newbold, this Convair 880-22M, N58RD visited Prestwick in September 1976, carrying oil-related passengers via Houston, Texas, to Daharan. It was later destroyed during American FAA crash tests in October 1986. (Peter Berry)

The Spanish-built CASA.352L version of the German Ju.52/3m, had served with the Spanish Air Force. Shown in transit at Prestwick in November 1979, N99069 was flown to the United States for display at the Southern Lake Michigan Wing of the Confederate Air Force. (Peter Berry)

A Rolls-Royce Merlin-powered copy of the Heinkel He.111, CASA 2.111E, N72615, flown by the Spanish Air Force, is shown in transit at Prestwick in October 1977, en route to the Confederate Air Force in Midland, Texas. (Peter Berry)

freighters. British Airways, having now taken over BOAC and BEA, opened a scheduled service to Toronto on 27 May. From 13 June, Aviaco began Inclusive Tour services to Palma, with Sud Caravelles.

During March and April 1975, Prestwick handled some 300 continental and domestic flights, due to industrial action at Glasgow. In August, an ex-Indian Air Force Consolidated B-24 Liberator, 250551, landing on Runway 31, suffered a collapsed nose-wheel. Scottish Aviation was able to affect a prompt repair. A further Air Show was held at the Airport in June. In October, Prestwick accepted another 101 weather diversions from adjacent airports.

Sixty-eight charter flights brought 11,000 French and German football fans to Prestwick on 12 May 1976, for the European Cup Final between Bayern Munich and St Etienne. British Airways began a Belfast–Prestwick–Edinburgh–Aberdeen service. On 7 July, PanAm began a four-times-weekly air-cargo service with Boeing 747.

Airliner crew training is a continuing feature at Prestwick, but a serious accident occurred on 17 March 1977, when a British Airtours Boeing 707, G-APFK, crashed on take-off from Runway 13, coming to rest near the tower and fire station. The airliner was written-off, but the three crew members escaped. Air Canada introduced Tristars and B747s on their Prestwick schedules from 24 April and Wardair began a weekly B747 ABC charter service to Toronto on 30 April.

The following February saw the first British Airways BAC Concorde training flights at Prestwick and on the 11th, Northwest added a Boston to Copenhagen B747 cargo service to its Prestwick operation. In March 1978, British Airways withdrew their domestic feeder flights through Prestwick, due to lack of passengers.

Consolidated B-24J Liberator B.VIII, N94459, had previously flown with the RAF as KH401 and the Indian Air Force as HE771. Now marked '250551', it suffered a collapsed nose-wheel, landing on Runway 31 at Prestwick in August, 1975. Liberator experts from British Aerospace were able to make a timely repair, before the flight continued to the United States. This Liberator was later used in the film *The Lost Prince* and was last reported at the Liberal Air Museum, Kansas. (Peter Berry)

The last of sixteen Anglo/French Concordes to be completed, G-BOAF is shown at Prestwick in June 1981, while on one of many crew training flights. She is now displayed at Filton. (Peter Berry)

British Caledonian began an air-cargo service through Prestwick. April saw the introduction of Airport Security Taxes, Super APEX, cheap budget and standby fares. In May, Quebec Air operated the first of several charter flights to Toronto. From 9 June, Northwest Airlines inaugurated a daily Copenhagen to Seattle service, via Prestwick, Boston and Minneapolis, with B747 and later DC-10 transports. British Airways began Boeing 737 training flights in September 1978.

From January, 1979, PanAmerican Airlines withdrew its air-cargo services from Prestwick and the last Air Canada flight from Prestwick to Gander departed on 24 April, ceasing the transatlantic services that began in 1943. Northwest began a B747 scheduled service to Boston. A further Prestwick Air Show was held on 2 June.

In 1980, British Caledonian and Laker opened charter services from Prestwick to Los Angeles and Miami. Air-cargo services at Prestwick received an increase in August 1981, when Flying Tigers introduced a weekly scheduled DC-8F service between Prestwick and New York. This was joined by a B747F service in 1982.

In January 1982, airlines operating through Prestwick were noted as: Laker and Wardair (DC-10), Northwest (B747/B747F), Flying Tiger (DC-8F/B747F), British Airtours (L101), Air Canada (L101/DC-8/DC-8F), World, Canadian Pacific, Transamerica (DC-8), Arrow Air (B707), British Airways (B747) and British Caledonian (DC-10/B707F).

RAFA again staged a Prestwick Air Show in June 1983, attracting more than 100,000 people. Some £25,000 was distributed to local charities. In August 1983, British Airways severed their forty-three-year-long links with Prestwick, when they terminated their services, adding their Scottish transatlantic passengers to the Glasgow–Heathrow 'Shuttle'.

Named *W.R. Wop May* (a Canadian pioneer aviator), Wardair Douglas DC-10-30, C-GXRC, is shown arriving at Prestwick with passengers on an Inclusive Tour charter flight. (Peter Berry)

Remembering the many RAFA Air Shows, here the Red Arrows grace the skies over Prestwick Airport. (Peter Berry)

'Open Skies'

The first thoughts of an 'Open Skies' policy for Scottish air transport had been discussed during 1984. In February, there were only three passenger flights each week, a Northwest B747 to Boston, an Air Canada Tristar to Toronto and an Air Canada DC-8 to Halifax. Air-cargo service was a once-weekly Flying Tiger B747F and one Air Canada DC-8F.

From 20 May 1985, Air Canada began a Prestwick to Halifax and Toronto service with B767s. Passenger charter flights continued through Prestwick and in 1986 services to Boston, Chicago and New York were being flown by American Transair (L101), Prestwick to Toronto by British Airtours (L101), Prestwick to Toronto and Winnipeg by Nationair (DC-8-63), Prestwick to Toronto by Quebec Air (DC-8-63), Prestwick to Toronto, Calgary and Vancouver by Wardair (B747) and Prestwick to Toronto and Vancouver by Worldways (DC-8-63 and L101).

Highland Express attempted a B747 service from Birmingham and Prestwick to New York in 1987, but went into liquidation after only five months of operations. In transit through the decade, was a DH.98 Mosquito, Boeing B-17F Fortress, and a Gulfstream 1.

Taxying for departure on Runway 31 at Prestwick in 1986, Air Canada Boeing 767, C-GAVC, '611', was bound for Toronto. (Peter Berry)

An unusual visitor to Prestwick in August 1989, was a Grumman Gulfstream 1, N5VX, from the Massachusetts Institute of Technology. It carried out flights over the Scottish Lochs with radar wave-sensing equipment. (Peter Berry)

The withdrawal of Scottish Gateway status from Prestwick in May 1990 saw Northwest Airlines moving their Prestwick–Boston service to Abbotsinch, followed by the Air Canada service to Toronto. British Airways opened a Glasgow to New York service and American Airlines opened Glasgow to Chicago. United and Wardair also served North America from Glasgow and the run-down of the airport began. With the closing of the Holy Loch nuclear-submarine base, the last USAF MATS charter flight departed in October 1991, the base closing the following March. With the withdrawal of Canadian Armed Forces from Europe, it was announced that CAF transit flights would continue to use Prestwick as their forward strategic staging post in Europe, which continues today.

Interesting Warbirds continued to transit Prestwick in the 1990s, the Liberator *Diamond L'il*, a MATS C-121A Constellation and Douglas C-54A Skymaster. An unexpected arrival was a round-the-world Cessna 206 Stationair, which alighted in Ayr Harbour, seeking fuel.

A Consolidated B-24, Liberator I, should have been delivered to Prestwick as AM927, in 1941, but was damaged before delivery. It was flown as a company transport during the war years and then purchased by the Confederate Air Force in 1968. It is pictured here in transit at Prestwick in July 1992. Marked N24927 and named *Diamond L'il*, she arrived just fifty-one years late! (Peter Berry)

During a round-the-world flight in July 1990, a Cessna 206 Stationair seaplane, N1990L, alighted in Ayr Harbour for fuel. Re-fuelling was completed from a Prestwick Airport tanker and the flight left next day. (Peter Berry)

The RAFA continued to find sponsors for the bi-annual Prestwick Air Show, until 1992 when the rising costs of ground services, insurance and buying-in flights reduced any worthwhile monies available for distribution to the local charities.

Air Canada cargo flights gained traffic rights from Prestwick to Zurich and Dusseldorf and air cargo at the airport totalled 12,000 tonnes in 1992, with terminal passengers reaching an all-time low of 11,000. A new west fire station was opened in December 1992, as was an Apron Services Building.

At the end of 1993, regular air-cargo services from Prestwick were noted by Federal Express B747, Air Canada DC-8F and Polar Air Cargo B747F, the total lift being 21,000 tonnes, with additional cargo and passengers charters. The Air Canada DC-8F cargo service through Prestwick was terminated on 26 March 1994, their cargo being 'roaded' to Glasgow to join their passenger services to Toronto. A new cargo service by Cargolux B747F freighters, from Luxembourg to Seattle, was begun two days later. Lufthansa also began a Frankfurt to Chicago service on 25 April with a B747F.

Ryanair Dublin–Prestwick

The long-awaited continental and domestic passenger services from Prestwick began on 3 May 1994, when Ryanair opened a twice-daily service from Dublin to Prestwick with Boeing 737-200 aircraft. This service increased to three services daily from the following May. The railway station and the air bridge to the terminal building were opened on 5 September.

Prestwick maintained its reputation as a weather diversion airport, when eighteen flights were diverted on 27 January 1995, from Abbotsinch, Edinburgh

Shown in service on the apron at Prestwick, Boeing 737-2T5, EI-CON, was part of the early fleet of Ryanair jetliners that introduced budget air fares to Scotland. (Peter Berry)

and Aberdeen. In addition to its scheduled air-cargo services by Cargolux, Lufthansa and Federal Express, passenger charter traffic during the summer of 1995 was provided by American Trans Air (L101), Air Transat (L101/B757) and Caledonian (A320). A three-times-daily service between Belfast and Prestwick was commenced by Gill Airways from 3 July and from 27 October Ryanair began a four-times-daily service between Prestwick and London/Stansted. These services attracted a healthy response from the travelling public.

By October 1995, sixty-eight services a week were scheduled between Prestwick, Dublin, London and Belfast, and by March 1996 passenger totals through the airport increased to 340,000, including 65,000 passengers between Dublin, 50,000 between Belfast and 225,000 between Prestwick and Stansted. Regular air-cargo flights by Cargolux, Lufthansa and Federal Express carried some 39,500 tonnes.

These improvements continued in 1996, with Laker Airways returning to the Prestwick to Orlando route in May. It was noted that on 20 May sixty-two arrival and departures were scheduled each day, from Laker (DC-10), Cargolux (B747), Ryanair (B737), Air Transat (L101), Gill (SD360), Fedex (MD11), Futura International (FUA), Transwede (TWE) and Lufthansa (B747s). In December the following services were logged during the month: Air France–6, B747F, Cargolux–17, B747F, Lufthansa–11, B747F, Federal Express–27, DC-10/MD11/B727, Gill–74, SD360/ATR42/ATR72, Ryanair–175, B737. By March 1997, Prestwick had recorded 542,000 passengers and 36,000 tonnes of air cargo.

From 24 April 1997, Ryanair based a B737 at Prestwick and began a 0650-timed business flight to London/Stansted. More than 560,000 passengers used the Prestwick Terminal to March 1998 and air cargo totalled 49,000 tonnes.

By March 1998, Prestwick Airport had returned to 24-hour operations and from 13 April the Stagecoach transport conglomerate acquired a holding in Glasgow/Prestwick. Daily services continued to Belfast, with Gill Airways by Ryanair, Dublin/4 and Stansted/5. Summer charters were offered to Bulgaria by Air Via, Jersey by Brymon, Ibiza and Majorca by Air Europe, Majorca by Air Futura, Turkey by Pegasus, Detroit and Florida by American Transair and Toronto by Air Transat. Air cargo services totalled forty-eight weekly, with Cargolux/16, Fedex/14, Air France/8 and Polar Air Cargo/4.

New training contracts at the airport saw the addition of the USAF C-20A/Learjet 35A and C-21A/Gulfstream 3 & 4 military transports as well as airline types from British Midland and Virgin Airlines. On 19 November 1998 Ryanair opened a Prestwick to Paris/Beauvais service. Terminal passengers to March 1999 totalled 547,000 and air cargo reached 50,000 tonnes.

Ryanair added a daily service from Prestwick to Frankfurt/Hahn on 26 March 2000 and from 27 June Corporate Jets operated one Learjet 31 business jet from Prestwick, later replaced by two Learjet 60s. Weekly air cargo services were Cargolux/6, Swiss Global/3, Air France/3, Polar Air Cargo/5 and Singapore/1.

Pictured at Prestwick in 1999, Cargolux Boeing B747F-121, LX-GCV, is a frequent visitor to the new air-cargo village. (Peter Berry)

Departing Prestwick in April 2000, Federal Express McDonnell Douglas, MD-11F, N612FE, named *Alyssa*, was on a scheduled service to North America. (Peter Berry)

Prestwick has always been in demand for airline crew training, and shown here is a Virgin Atlantic, Boeing 747-219B, G-VZZZ, named *Morning Glory*, climbing away after another 'touch-and-go'. (Peter Berry)

Providing the busy executive with high-speed air transport, Prestwick is home to Learjet 60 business-jets, this one, N139XX, preparing for departure in 1999. (Peter Berry)

Shown arriving at the Prestwick Terminal in 2004, Ryanair Boeing 737-800, EI-CTB, joins its three locally based aircraft for another busy day serving fifteen destinations from Prestwick Airport. (Alistair Firth)

Ryanair services from Prestwick in 2001 introduced the 189-seat, Boeing 737-800 series, a fleet of which will gradually replace the earlier Boeing model. Daily flights totalled nine to London/Stansted, four daily flights to Dublin, two flights a day to Paris/Beauvais and a daily service to Frankfurt/Hann. From 26 April, an additional daily service was begun to Brussels/Charleroi. More than 1 million passengers used the terminal building during the previous twelve months and 41,000 tonnes of air cargo were handled at the air cargo centre. By 30 April 2001, airport revenue totalled £25 million, 55 per cent from passengers, 30 per cent from air cargo and 15 per cent from general aviation, property and maintenance.

Ryanair began daily services to Oslo/Torp on 4 April 2002 and during the winter Ryanair flew daily services to London/Stansted/8, Dublin/4, Paris/2, Frankfurt/1, Bussels/1 and Oslo/1. Terminal passengers to March 2002 totalled 1.2 million, with 43,000 tonnes of air cargo lifted.

A twice-daily service to Bournemouth was opened by Ryanair in March 2003. Globespan began operations on 1 April, with weekly flights to Malaga/2, Nice/2, Rome/2 and Palma/7. Aer Arran Express began daily flights to the Isle of Man from 21 May. The following day, Ryanair opened a daily service to Barcelona/Gerona. From 28 July 2003, BMIbaby moved their Glasgow to Cardiff service to Prestwick. Ryanair added daily flights to Stockholm/Skavsta and Bournemouth and from 16 October to Gothenburg. From December a service was begun to Shannon and four 189-seat Boeing 737-800 aircraft were now based at Prestwick. More than 1.97 million passengers had used the terminal building to March 2004.

In January, 2004, Ryanair continued additional services from Prestwick with a daily service to Milan, and on 3 May, their tenth anniversary at Prestwick, opened a further service to Rome/Ciampino. In addition, for the summer,

Departing Prestwick on 25 September, 2003, with a cargo for New York, Antonov 225 Mriya, UR-82060, the world's largest transport, sports six turbofan engines, fourteen double-wheel bogies, a span of 290ft and a gross weight at take-off, of 600,000kg (1,323,000lb). (Fred Seggie)

Ryanair scheduled daily flights to London/Stansted/5, Dublin/3, Paris/2, as well as flights to/from Oslo, Gothenburg, Bournemouth, Milan/Gerona, Frankfurt/Hahn, Brussels/Charloi, Shannon and Stockholm. Aer Arann opened a twice-weekly service to Donegal on 3 May, with ATR-42 transports increasing to three services a week in June. Air Wales replaced BMIbaby in April, with twice-daily flights to Cardiff. Ryanair also opened a service to Donegal. Air Caledonia opened service to the City of Derry daily service, except Saturdays to Stornoway. On 8 September, Ryanair announced four new destinations from Prestwick, daily services to Dusseldorf from November and from March 2005, services to Hamburg, Pisa and Murcia, near Alicante.

Weekly charter flights continued with flights to Alicante, Faro, Ibiza and Gran Canaria. The 2005 season would add Majorca, Orlando, Teneriffe, Arrefife and Bulgaria. Two Short SC.5 Belfast cargo transports were resident at Prestwick during the year. The Russian operator, Polet Cargo Airlines, flying the large and heavy Antonov 124, continued using Prestwick for their westbound charter services. The return of transatlantic scheduled services from Prestwick began on 12 April 2005, when British West Indian Airlines, opened a Manchester–Prestwick–Barbados–Port of Spain service with Airbus A340-300 transports.

Restoring transatlantic air services to Prestwick, British West Indian Airways Airbus A340 touches down on 2 April 2005, en route to Barbados and Trinidad. (Peter Berry)

Chapter Five

Air Traffic Control Centres, 1959–2004

Following the wartime years and early post-war period already described, a combined Scottish Airways and Prestwick oceanic operations room was opened in 1959, together with their associated 'fixed' and 'mobile' telecommunication centres, occupying the wartime Seco-huts, adjacent to Redbrae House. The oceanic

Shown in 1963, this control desk was first used in 1959, to manage the oceanic air traffic over the North Atlantic. Long-range radio and teleprinter machines kept the controllers updated on the progress of flights. (CAA)

control desk with its flight progress strip bays and communication panels was backed by teleprinters, accepting flight plans and movement messages as well as accepting messages from the Prestwick and the Shanwick Aeradio station near Shannon. A traffic dispatch position was sited nearby for the sending of controller messages to transatlantic aircraft via the two, long-range, HF R/T radio stations. The Scottish Airways position, controlling flights over Scotland and the North Sea, was on a raised dais and carried Sector One (Dean Cross and Talla), Sector Two (Machrihanish and Skipness) and Sector Five (Flight Information Region) positions.

The National Air Traffic Service (NATS) was established by the Ministry of Civil Aviation in 1962, to provide a common system of control for both civil and military air traffic. NATS was taken under the 'umbrella' of the Civil Aviation Authority (CAA) in 1972, controlling and regulating air services in the UK.

The first civil ATC radar to operate in Scotland came into service in 1963, when the Ministry of Civil Aviation(MCA) took over the RAF long-range radar station at Gailes on the Ayrshire coast. The station worked in conjunction with the procedural 'D' controllers at the Redbrae Centre. A long-range Secondary Surveillance Radar (SSR), with a link into the Redbrae Airways operation room, was installed at Stornoway in 1970, providing positive cover to transponder-equipped air traffic over a large part of Scotland.

The increases in transatlantic crossings to 68,191 in 1964 and the replacement of the last of the propeller transports by turbo-jets, showed the need for a consistent, specialist approach to the provision of both communication and air traffic services. The ICAO Council in Montreal therefore agreed to establish a permanent North Atlantic Systems Planning Group (NAT SPG) on

Scottish Airways radar station at Gailes, on the Ayrshire coast, provided the radar 'eyes' for the 'D' controllers at Redbrae. The radar controllers at the Gailes were equipped with Type 7, Type 14 High and Low, radar pictures. (Peter Berry)

15 April 1965, based in the Paris office. At their first meeting in October 1965, two major changes in the direction of the control and communication responsibilities took place. The first of these was that the North Atlantic ground-air-ground communication service was to be provided by Shanwick Aeradio Station, Shannon, and the complementary air traffic control service was to be provided by Shanwick Control at Prestwick, who assumed the responsibility for the control of all air traffic in the eastern part of the North Atlantic. In particular, they issued clearances to all westbound transatlantic flights, planning to cross the Eastern Shanwick OCA boundary, within latitudes 45N to 61N.

Oceanic Air Traffic Control to Atlantic House

Transatlantic ATC remained at Redbrae House in Scotland for thirty-one years, until 5 April 1972, when the Oceanic Control Centre moved down the road to Atlantic House, the re-furbished National Coal Board building in the town of Prestwick. The improved inter-centre communications and the first use of computers to prepare flight progress strips soon matched the improved working environment. Following trials, the on-line data interchange (OLDI) of east and westbound flight data, between the Apollo computer at Prestwick and the GAATS computer at Gander was begun in 1975.

Having pioneered the use of digital computers for ATC purposes since 1961, the Prestwick Oceanic operation made another bold step forward on 31 March 1987, when Apollo was replaced by a real-time, Flight Data Processing System,

Purchased from, but never used by, the National Coal Board in the town of Prestwick, the Civil Aviation Authority transferred the Oceanic Control Centre from Redbrae here in 1972. Scottish Airways, Radar and the RAF Control Centre followed in 1978. (Peter Berry)

Shown here is the Oceanic Control Operations Room at Atlantic House, Prestwick, following the move from Redbrae in 1972. The small computer screen on the left was linked to the Apollo computer, used for calculating data for transatlantic flights. The software was 8k! (Peter Berry)

(OACC FDPS). The most radical change was the replacement of the ATC flight progress strip, with an on-screen, electronic presentation. A computer link was established to Shanwick Aeradio at Shannon, to allow the direct entry of position reports, filed by transatlantic en route aircraft. The OLDI links were extended to adjacent ATC agencies in Iceland, the Azores, the UK, Ireland, France and Spain. While telephone facilities are still provided, their use for passing routine ATC information is rare.

Perhaps the most striking area of automation has occurred with the interfaces between the flight deck and Shanwick Control at Prestwick. Trials of passing clearances directly from Oceanic FDPS to the flight deck of suitably equipped aircraft began in 1989. In 2004, approximately 70 per cent of westbound flights, approaching the eastern boundary, receive their North Atlantic clearance without a word being passed by voice. Also in 2004, some 30 per cent of flights are filing their en route position reports directly into Oceanic FDPS, using satellite-based, data-link technology. In 2003, Shanwick Control at Prestwick handled 339,524 oceanic flights. The current daily record of 1,189 was set on 10 September 2004, when aircraft were crossing the eastern boundary at a peak rate of around 118 flights an hour. This equates to some 400 turbo-jet transports en route, over the North Atlantic at peak times.

Left: Following the introduction of Oceanic Flight Data Processing System in 1987, controllers are seen managing the busy North Atlantic airspace, east of 30 degrees west. (CAA)

Below: From 1989, Oceanic FDPS was able to send oceanic clearances via data-link, from Prestwick, direct to the transatlantic aircraft flight deck. (Lockheed)

Scottish Airways Centre to Atlantic House

The Scottish Airways Centre moved into Atlantic House on the completion of the purpose-built extension on 2 November 1978. For the first time, procedural controllers, previously located at Redbrae, worked side-by-side with their radar colleagues, who had previously worked in the old radar station at Gailes. The Scottish Military Air Traffic Control Centre, ScATCC (MiL), the RAF D&D Cell and ADNC also moved to Atlantic House and joined the Scottish Airway Controllers in their new Operations Room.

The new facilities in Atlantic House featured a fully processed Marconi LOCUS radar display system and voice communications facilities. Like the oceanic environment, the Scottish Airways operation would need constant enhancement to meet significant traffic growth – not only from overflying North Atlantic traffic, but also due to large increases in the use of Scottish airports.

A total of thirteen radar pictures are now linked into the Scottish Airways Centre. In 1994, computer-generated flight strips were provided, albeit derived from the National Airspace System (NAS) located at West Drayton Centre, London. By the late 1990s, it was clear that the LOCUS system was unable to cope with the air traffic demand, leading to its replacement by a Lockheed-Martin Skyline system.

Following their move from Gailes and Redbrae to Atlantic House, the Scottish Area Radar controllers were repositioned alongside their Airway 'D' controllers. (CAA)

The National Air Traffic Services became a separate limited company (NATS Ltd) from the Civil Aviation Authority in July, 2001.

The airways operation has coped with the traffic by increasing the number of sector positions. During 2003, a significant redesign of North Sea airspace led to the airspace controlled from Prestwick extending south as far as the Humber Estuary. There are currently thirteen civil sectors within the Scottish Airways operations room, plus the FIR position – the only remaining procedural element from Redbrae days. During 2003, the Scottish Airways operation controlled 543,454 flights. The current daily record movements occurred on 16 July 2004, when 2,127 flights were handled.

The Future of the Prestwick Site

By 2006, the oceanic operation will have used its FDPS computer for nineteen years and will be replaced by a collaboration development with the Canadian North Atlantic ATC provider, Nav Canada. The replacement SAATS System is expected to enter service in a purpose-built, interim operations room during 2006.

The Scottish Airways operation forms part of the national 'Two Centre Strategy', along with the recently opened Swanwick Centre, near Southampton.

Presently under construction, the new Prestwick Air Traffic Control Centre confirms the twin strategy of two ATCCs in the UK at Swanwick and Prestwick, each safeguarding the other. Scottish Airways and Scottish (Mil), will occupy the building towards the end of the decade, with the Oceanic Control Centre following. (NATS)

The existing operations room at Prestwick is close to capacity and a replacement facility is under construction, adjacent to Atlantic House. This Prstwick Centre will house the Scottish Airways operation and also the current Manchester Control Centre, which will close. The new facility is expected to open in 2009. The Shanwick Oceanic Operation is expected to share the operations room with Scottish Airways in 2011 for the first time since the two were separated at Redbrae in 1967.

Appendix One

Tiger Moth Fleet at No.12 E&RFTS Prestwick 1936/39

The Tiger Moth, G-ADUC, was registered on 10 October 1935, and was impressed as BB812.
Eighteen Tiger Moths were registered on 9 December 1935:

G-ADHN	BB811	G-ADVX	BB799	G-ADVY	BB795
G-ADVZ	BB796	G-ADWA	BB797	G-ADWB	BB798
G-ADWC	BB794	G-ADWE	BB800	G-ADWF	BB801
G-ADWJ	BB803	G-ADWK	BB802	G-ADWL	BB804
G-ADWM	BB805	G-ADWN	BB808	G-ADWO	BB807
G-ADWP	BB806	G-ADYA	BB810	G-ADYB	BB809

The Tiger Moth, G-AFFA, was registered on 28 August 1938 and was impressed as BB813.
The Tiger Moth, G-AFWI, was registered 19 July 1939 and was impressed as BB814.
From 3 September 1939, as No.12 EFTS, the Tiger Moths are recorded above, as well as Tiger Moth L6932, and codes used for aircraft were numbered 1 to 54.
All the Tiger Moths were impressed into the RAF on 12 October 1940.

Other aircraft types recorded are:

Tiger Moth L6933 Hart K2459 Demon K2842,
Audax K3077 Anson L7948
Battle K7607 Hind K5419

The two Fokker F.XXIIs and single Fokker F.XXXVI, purchased in 1939, were flown by No.12 EFTS and No.1 AONS, under civil registrations until impressed into the RAF in October 1941.

G-AFXR	Registered, 9 August 1939. Ex PH-AJR/HM159. Caught fire in the air and crashed in Loch Tarbet, 1 July 1943.
G-AFZP	Registered, 15 August 1939. Ex PH-AJP/HM160. Stored in 1943, re-registered for Scottish Airlines, as G-AFZP in 1946,.
G-AFZR	Registered, 15 August 1939. Ex PH-AJA/HM161. Lost power on take-off and overshot, Prestwick, 21 May 1940. Not repaired, serial not used.

Appendix Two

Dates of First Transatlantic Arrivals at Prestwick/Largs/Greenock

Royal Air Force

Catalina	13 July 1939	P9630
Catalina	26 October 1940	AM258
Hudson	11 November 1940	T9422
Liberator	14 March 1941	AM259
Fortress	14 April 1941	AN534
Lodestar	9 July 1941	NC34901/No.2087
Commando	12 November 1941	G-AGDI
Ventura/B-34	15 April 1942	AE691/762
Mitchell	16 May 1942	FK162
Marauder	2 September 1942	FK138
Boston	12 October 1942	BZ199/203/220
Dakota	11 February 1943	FD769
Ventura/PV-1	9 April 1943	FN956
Coronado	24 April 1943	JX470
Hadrian	1 July 1943	FR579
Mariner	19 August 1943	JX103
Mosquito	8 August 1943	KB162
Lancaster	19 September 1943	KB700
York	19 October 1943	MW100
Baltimore	22 May 1944	FW302
Skymaster	10 June 1944	EW999
Stirling	26 June 1944	LK584
Spitfire	11 July 1944	MK210/317

USAAF/USN

B-24	3 July 1941	AC40-702
B307	18 April 1942	NC19908
C-87	20 June 1942	American A/L
B-17	1 July 1942	AF41-9085
C-47	1 July 1942	AF41-7833
P-38	8 July 1942	AF41-7561
PBY	9 July 1942	'5AJ-73'
C-53	15 July 1942	AF41-20095
B-26	26 July 1942	AF41-1042
B-25	24 September 1942	AF41-13048
A-20	24 September 1942	AF41-3031
C-54	10 October 1942	AF41-20141
PV-1	9 April 1943	Bu.33072
R5D	6 May 1943	Bu.39137
F-5A	7 July 1943	AF41-3317
C-60A	11 July 1943	AF42-56018
P-47	11 August 1943	AF42-8570
PB4Y	17 August 1943	Bu.*****
AT-23	2 May 1944	AF*****
YB-29	7 March 1944	AF41-36963
PB2Y-3R	18 May 1944	NC7219
C-46	12 June 1944	AF*****
A-26	9 June 1944	AF*****
F-8	23 July 1944	AF****
F-3A	5 September 1944	AF*****
C-109	8 October, 1944	AF*****

Appendix Three

Numbers of Aircraft Delivered to the RAF over the North Atlantic

Catalina	550
Mariner	27
Coronado	10
Liberator	637
Hudson	809
Fortress	179
Ventura	199
Mitchell	654
Marauder	8
Lodestar	12
Boston	313
Hadrian	1
Dakota	769
Baltimore	1
Lancaster	314
Electra	1
Skymaster	3
Mosquito	437
	Total=4,924

Ref: Cumulative Receipts & Deliveries, No.45 Group, RAF
September 1940 to April 1945
PRO File A.38/23

Records held by Trans-Atlantic Control (TAC), from October 1940 to April 1945, show the total flights controlled over the North Atlantic by the Centre at Gloucester and Prestwick as:

1940	26 }
1941	805 }
1942	2,436 }
1943	6,817 }
1944	16,224 }
1945	11,736 }
	Total=38,044

Records held in the National Archives at Kew, London, show the following:

RAF Deliveries to the UK, N&S Atlantic	5,793 }
Transport and Weather flights	15,808 }
USAAF deliveries	15,041 }
USN flights	731 }
RCAF flights	386 }
Miscellaneous	67 }
	Total=37,826

The author's further research has shown that at least 340 flights were lost over the North Atlantic during the five years of war.

Appendix Four

Dates of Military Units at Prestwick

Unit	In	From	Out	To	Aircraft
12E&RFTS	17.02.36	Formed	03.09.39	12 EFTS	Tiger Moth Hart & Hind Fokker & Anson Battle
1 CANS	15.08.38	Formed	01.11.39	1 AONS	Anson
12 EFTS	03.09.39	12 E&RFTS	22.03.41	Disbanded	Tiger Moth
2 SofW/T	??.09.39	Opened	15.10.40	Closed	*****
1 AONS	01.11.39	1 CANS	19.07.41	Disbanded	Fokker & Anson
10 AONS	27.11.39	Grangemouth	02.12.39	1 AONS	Anson
603	16.12.39	Turnhouse	16.01.40	Dyce & Montrose	Spitfire
610	04.04.40	Wittering	09.05.40	Biggin Hill	Spitfire
825 RN	21.04.40	HMS *Glorious*	03.05.40	Worthy Down	Swordfish
141	21.07.40	West Malling	21.08.40	Dyce & Montrose	Defiant
1COTU	09.08.40	Silloth	01.11.40	Catfoss	Blenheim
253	23.08.40	Turnhouse	28.08.40	Kenley	Hurricane
615	29.08.40	Kenley	09.10.40	Kenley	Hurricane
102	01.09.40	Leeming	09.10.42	Linton-on Ouse	Whitley
4 FPP ATA	15.09.40	Formed	13.10.45	Disbanded	Anson & Argus
AI/ASV School	24.10.40	Formed	27.12.40	3 Radio School	Blenheim
1 RCAF	10.10.40	Northolt	07.12.40	Castletown	Hurricane
602	17.12.40	Prestwick	15.04.41	Ayr	Spitfire
800 RN	27.10.40	Crail	30.10.40	HMS *Ark Royal*	Roc?
821X RN	15.12.40	Donibristle	16.12.40	Donibristle	Swordfish
3 Radio School	27.12.40	Formed	19.08.42	3 RDF School	Botha
807 RN	04.02.41	Yeovilton	06.02.41	Abbotsinch	Fulmar
1527BATFlt	29.10.41	Formed	28.02.46	Disbanded Oxford	Hudson
1425Flt	30.10.41	Formed	05.04.42	Lyneham	Liberator
3 RDF School	19.08.42	Above	01.12.42	Hooton Park	Blenheim
1680Flt	06.03.44	Abbotsinch	07.02.46	Disbanded	Dominie Fokker & Anson
825 RN	21.04.40	HMS *Glorious*	03.05.40	Worthy Down	Swordfish
800 RN	27.10.40	Crail	30.10.40	HMS *Ark Royal*	Roc?
821X RN	15.12.40	Donibristle	16.12.40	Donibristle	Swordfish
807 RN	04.02.41	Yeovilton	06.02.41	Abbotsinch	Fulmar

Unit	In	From	Out	To	Aircraft
HMS *Gannet*	23.11.70	Prestwick			
819 RN	27.10.71	Culdrose	01.11.01		Sea King
845 RN	24.10.73	Culdrose (Dt2)	26.10.73		Sea King
820 RN	24.05.77	Culdrose (Dt2)	03.06.77	Culdrose	Sea King
814 RN	11.06.81	Culdrose (Dt2)	03.07.81		Sea King
826 RN	05.09.82	Culdrose (Dt2)	29.09.82		Sea King
810 RN	13.02.84	Culdrose (Dt4)	?		Sea King
RNAS Prestwick	??01.94	SAR Flt	07.01.02	Current	Sea King

Appendix Five

BOAC Fleet of Return Ferry Service Liberators

LB-30A Liberator

No.1 AM258 — Delivered St Hubert, Montreal–Gander–Prestwick,4/5 May 1941. Capt. D.C.T Bennett. First Eastbound RFS service. Veered off Runway 26 at Prestwick on 13 September 1943 and crashed into the Pow Burn, partially burnt out.

No.2 AM259 — Delivered St Hubert–Gander–Squires Gate, 13/14 March 1941. Wg Cdr Waghorn. First RFS Delivery. Flown as G-AGCD/AM259. SOC Dorval, 7 November 1945.

No.3 AM260 — Delivered St Hubert–Gander–Squires Gate, 5/6 April 1941. Capt. Youell. Cracks found in tailplane at Gander on 28 March. Tailplane of AM915 fitted. First westbound BOAC RFS service from Squires Gate, 4 May 1941. Crashed on take-off, departing Ayr/Heathfield for Gander, 14 August 1941. Twenty-two killed. Capt. R. Stafford.

No.4 AM261 — Delivered St Hubert–Gander–Prestwick, 2 June 1941. Capt. Allen. After take-off from Ayr/Heathfield for 10 Gander 10 August, 1941, flew into Goat Fell, Isle of Arran, twenty-two killed. Capt. E.R.B. White.

No.5 AM262 — Delivered St Hubert–Gander–Ayr/Heathfield, 26/27 May 1941. Capt. Page. Completed 1,000th RFS crossing on 7 September 1944.

No.6 AM263 — Delivered St Hubert–Gander–Prestwick, 2 June 1941. Capt. Messenger. Collided with Dakota, FZ637 at Lagens, 30 November 1944. DBR.

LB-30B Liberator I

No.6 AM915 — Delivered St Hubert–Gander–Prestwick, 5 August 1941. Crashed en route Gander–Prestwick. 1 September 1941. Capt. K.D. Garden BOAC. While diverting to Squires Gate due to weather, descended through cloud and at 700ft hit Achinoan Hill near Campbeltown on the Mull of Kintyre. All ten killed.

No.9 AM918 — Delivered New York–Gander–Prestwick, 13/14 May 1941. Capt. Cripps. Registered G-AGDR, 5 January 1942. Inaugurated Prestwick–Hurn–Cairo service 24/26 January 1942. On return, shot down by friendly fire (a Polish night fighter) off The Eddystone

Light, England, 15 February 1942. Capt. Humphrey-Page. Nine killed. 'The flight was returning from Yalta, bringing the Minutes from the Conference. The only thing they found floating was the diplomatic bag'.

No.11 AM920 — Delivered New York–Gander–Prestwick, 13 May 1941. Capt. Bennett. Damaged in take-off accident, Dorval, 1 June 1943. Rebuilt with C-87 fuselage. Returned to BOAC December 1944. Registered G-AHYB, 19 August 1946. To SAL, April 1949. Out of service, 17 September 1949.

LB-30 Liberator II

No.5 AL507 — Delivered Gander–Prestwick, 16 March 1942. Registered G-AHYC, 29 August 1946. Departed Prestwick for Montreal, but u/c trouble. Damaged beyond repair, belly-landing at Ayr/Heathfield, 13 November 1946.

No.10 AL512 — Delivered Gander–Ayr, 15 October 1941. Hit snow drift and crashed on take-off, from Gander, 27 December 1943.

No.12 AL514 — Delivered and flown Prestwick–Montreal, 26 June 1942. Registered G-AGJP, 11 November 1943, but flown as AL514. To SAL, April, 1949.

No.20 AL522 — Delivered Gander–Ayr/Heathfield, 13 December 1941. To BOAC for the RFS, 1 August 1944. Registered G-AHYD, 19 August 1946. To SAL for re-fuelling modifications. Used for in-flight refuelling trials Montreal–Heathrow–Montreal, 4/5 February 1948.

No.26 AL528 — Delivered Montreal–Prestwick, 10 July 1942. Crashed landing in icing conditions, Charlottetown, PEI, 21/22 February 1946. Capt. D.W. Ray. Three crew injured, eight passengers safe.

No.27 AL529 — Delivered Montreal–Prestwick, 25/26 August 1942. Registered G-AHYE, 1 August 1946. Broken up at Prestwick, 7 December 1948.

No.89 AL591 — Delivered Gander–Prestwick, 25 July 1942. Ran out of fuel and crash landed on approach to Gander, 9 February 1943.

No.90 AL592 — Delivered Montreal–Prestwick, 16 August 1942. Registered G-AHYF, 19 August 1946. To SAL, April 1949. To F-BEFY.

No.95 AL597 — Delivered Gander–Prestwick, 14 December 1941. To BOAC for the RFS, 26 June 1944. Hit a snowdrift landing at Goose Bay from Montreal/Dorval on 16 January 1946.

No.101 AL603 — Delivered Gander–Prestwick, 6 May 1942. To BOAC for the RFS, 12 June 1944. Registered, G-AHYG, 29 August 1946. To SAL, April 1949. To F-BFGK, 21 April 1952.

No.112 AL614 — Delivered Gander–Prestwick, 2 September 1942. Broken up at Dorval, 30 June 1946.

No.123 AL625 — Delivered Gander–Prestwick, 4 May 1942. To BOAC for the RFS, 8 April 1944. Withdrawn, 15 July 1946. Broken up at Dorval, 23 May 1947.

No.125 AL627 — Delivered Gander–Prestwick, 2 July 1942. Broken up at Dorval, 23 May 1947.

Appendix Six

Prestwick Open Day, 15 September 1945

To celebrate the end of the Second World War, an 'Open Day' was staged at Prestwick on 15 September 1945. Among the aircraft that took part were:

Scottish Aviation Ltd	B-24 Liberator B-17 Fortress Fokker XXII Mosquito Dakota Lancaster Mk. X Glider
Air Transport Auxiliary	Halifax Warwick Lincoln Seafire Avenger Barracuda Sea Otter Hellcat Wildcat Argus Anson
No.1680 Flight, RAF	Walrus Dominie Wellington
MAEE	Boston
Royal Naval Air Service	Corsair
Air Ministry	Dakota Stirling, with airborne equipment Lancaster, operational Spitfire Mustang Typhoon

Ref: AIR.28/653.

Appendix Seven

Scottish Airline Fleet, 1945–1963

Type	Registration & c/n	Registered	Disposal
Fokker F.XXII	G-AFZP/HM160.	15 August 1939	Ex PH-ATP. Withdrawn at Prestwick, 10 August 1947
Dakota	G-AGWS/No.6208	18 December 1945	CF-FCQ, 18 July 1952
Dakota	G-AGZF /No.9172	18 December 1952	French Air Force, 15 October 1952
Dakota	G-AGZG/No.9803	11 January 1946	French Air Force, 1 November 1952
Dakota	G-AIOD /No.25292	14 October 1946	LX-LAB, 23 January 1948
Dakota	G-AIOE/No.12373	8 October 1946	SX-BAA, 1947, LX-LAC, 1 March 1948
Dakota	G-AIOF/No.12332	5 October 1946	SX-BBB, 9 March 1948
Dakota	G-AJBC/No.12304	18 October 1946	SX-BBC, 13 February 1948
Dakota	G-AJBD/No.13012	15 January 1947	SX-BBD, 15 February 1948
Dakota	G-AJLZ/No.10101	31 March 1947	LX-LAA, 31 December 1947
Dakota	G-AJVY/No.12358	4 February 1947	*London Express* Newspapers, 2 July 1948
Dakota	G-AKNM/No.25799	6 August 1947	Westminster Airways, 2 December 1947
Dakota	G-AMJU/No.25925	28 October 1954	Starways, 10 January 1955
Dakota	G-AMPP/No.26717	4 March 1952	Danair, 39, 30 March 1961
Liberators			
LB-30	G-AGZH/No.69/AL571	11 January 1946	Scrapped, Prestwick, April 1950
LB-30	G-AGZI/No.55/AL557	11 January 1946	SX-DAA, *Maid of Athens* February 1948
Mk.III	G-AHDY/No.27/LV337	27 February 1946	Scrapped at Prestwick, October 1950
LB-30	G-AHZP/No.14/AL516	19 July 1946	Crashed, landing Speke, 13 October 1948
LB-30	G-AHZR/No.50/AL552	19 July 1946	SX-DAB, December 1949
RFS Liberators operated by Scottish Airlines, April to September 1949			
LB-30	G-AGJP/No.12/AL514	11 November 1943	F-BEFX, April 1951
LB-30B	G-AHYB/No.11/AM920	19 August 194	F-BEFR, April 1951
LB-30	G-AHYD/No.20/AL522	19 August1946	F-BFGJ, May,1951
LB-30	G-AHYF/No.90/AL592	19 August 1946	F-BEFY, April 1951
LB-30	G-AHYG/No.101/AL603	29 August 1946	F-BFGK, April 1951

Type	Registration & c/n	Registered	Disposal
York	G-AMUL/MW308	18 September 1952	Crashed on t/o Stansted, 30 April 1956
York	G-AMUM/MW332	18 September 1952	Crashed landing, Luqa, 14 April 1954
York	G-AMUN/MW321	18 September 1952	Crashed approaching, Stansted,23 December 1957
York	G-ANSY/MW193	14 July 1954	Crashed on t/o Malta, 18 February 1956
York	G-ANRC/MW327	30 April 1954	Crashed on take-off, Stansted, 22 September 1954
York	G-ANVO/MW253	18 November 1954	Withdrawn, Luton, June 1963
York	G-ANYA/MW210	4 January 1955	Withdrawn at Stansted, August 1959
Oxford II	G-AHDZ/ED190	27 February 1946	F-BBIU, July 1954
Rapide	G-ALBH/X7490	7 June 1948	OO-CJD, September 1960
Rapide	G-ALBI/X7352	7 June 1948	F-OBRV, August 1960
Rapide	G-AKSF/R9562	2 February 1948	Destroyed by fire, Prestwick, 23 July 1949
PrOctoberor II	G-AHMP/BV631	9 May 1946	Withdrawn at Leavesden, April 1963
PrOctoberor II	G-AHMT/R7528	9 May 1946	Withdrawn at Prestwick, August 1948
Walrus	G-AJNP	10 April 1947	Scrapped at Prestwick, 28 August 1959
Walrus	G-AJNO	10 April 1947	Restored for Scottish Airlines. Cancelled
Tiger Moth	G-AJHR/DE315	12 February 1947	ZK-AUZ, August 1950

Appendix Eight

Scottish Airline Contracts, 1946–1956

Route		**Commenced**	**Completed**
Scottish Airlines Direct–DC-3			
Prestwick–Belfast	Scottish Airlines	28 January 1946	31 August 1946
Prestwick– Copenhagen–Faroes	Scottish Airlines	22 July 1946	14 October 1946
Scheduled Services under Contract – Liberator			
Reykjavik–Prestwick	Iceland Airways	27 May 1946	6 July 1948
Reykjavik–New York	Iceland Airways	16 September 1946	10 November 46
Prestwick–Montreal	BOAC RFS	4 April 1949	28 September 1949
Scheduled Services under Contract–DC-3			
Prestwick–Copenhagen	Iceland Airways	27 May 1946	6 July 1948
Prestwick–Amsterdam	Royal Dutch Airlines	29 July 1946	30 March 1947
Prestwick–Manchester–Paris	Air France	20 September 1946	28 February 1947
Prestwick–Renfrew–London	BEA		
Prestwick–London	BEA	(Varying periods between	
Renfrew–Belfast	BEA	2 September 1946–1 July 1947)	
London–Edinburgh–Aberdeen	BEA		
Under Associate Agreement with British European Airways–DC-3			
Prestwick–Isle-of-Man	BEA	1 June 1949	
Prestwick–Blackpool–Manchester	BEA	1 June 1949	3 September 1949
Prestwick–Burtonwood–London	BEA	8 June 1951	15 February 1953
Charter Contracts – 5x DC-3			
Delhi–Karachi	BOAC for Pakistan Government Evacuation of Pakistanis	23 August 1947	15 September 1947

Route		Commenced	Completed
Charter Contracts – 6x DC-3			
Agra–Lahore	BOAC for Indian Government Evacuation of Indians	14 October 1947	24 November 1947
Charter Contracts – 3 x Liberator, 2 x DC-3			
Belfast–Liverpool	Milk Marketing Board	20 August 1948	28 October 1948
Charter Contracts – Yorks			
London–Prestwick–Montreal	Trans Canada A/l. Transport of Cargo	7 March 1953	30 July 1953
Through Subsidiary Companies – DC-3			
Luxembourg–London–Prestwick	(Luxembourg A/l	2 February 1948	4 November 1949
Luxembourg–Frankfurt	(Luxembourg A/l	2 February 1948	4 November 1949
Luxembourg–Paris	(Luxembourg A/l	2 February 1948	4 November 1949
Luxembourg–Zurich	(Luxembourg A/l	2 February 1948	4 November 1949
Luxembourg–Lydda	(Luxembourg A/l	2 February 1948	4 November 1949
Brussels–Manchester–Prestwick	COBETA	17 July 1947	August 1948
Brussels–Lydda	COBETA		
Through Subsidiary Companies – Liberator, DC-4 & DC-3			
London–Paris–Rome-Athens Cairo	Hellenic Airlines	1 March 1948	30 June 1951
Athens–Cyprus–Lydda	Hellenic Airlines	1 March 1948	30 June 1951
Athens–Alexandria	Hellenic Airlines	1 March 1948	30 June 1951
Athens–Port Said	Hellenic Airlines	1 March 1948	30 June 1951
Eight Greek Internal Air Services	Hellenic Airlines	1 March 1948	30 June 1951
Air Ministry Contracts – 3 x Liberators & 2 x DC-3s			
Wunstorf/Fassberg/Schleswigland –Berlin	Fuel and supplies	11 June 1948	12 May 1949
Air Ministry Contracts – Yorks			
London–Prestwick–Montreal	Transport of passengers	15 November 1952	17 February 1957
Stansted–Fayid–Canal Zone	As above	1 August 1955	31 March 1956
Lyneham–Malta–Ed Adem–Nicosia	Transport of cargo	1 July 1956	

Appendix Nine

Prestwick Passenger and Cargo Traffic 1947–2004

Year 1 April/31 March	Passengers	Tonnes	Year	Passengers	Tonnes
1947/48	81,000		1976/77	400,056	14,544
1948/49	91,500		1977/78	386,156	19,191
1949/50	110,000		1978/79	363,772	20,636
1950/51	117,000		1979/80	417,907	20,684
1951/52	128,000	1,000	1980/81	387,168	20,122
1952/53	169,000		1981/82	351,411	16,191
1953/54	187,000		1982/83	255,100	11,400e
1954/55	195,000		1983/84	250,000	10,500e
1955/56	208,000		1984/85	236,000	10,700e
1956/57	243,000		1985/86	237,700	11,671
1957/58	260,000		1986/87	241,000	10,095
1958/59	218,500	1,215	1987/88	299,400	12,615
1959/60	243,600	1,589	1988/89	302,700	17,263
1960/61	301,000		1989/90	317,000	16,155e
1961/62	198,795	2,936	1990/91	95,000	13,918e
1962/63	194,524		1991/92	35,000	15,151e
1963/64	196,851	3,653	1992/93	11,000	16,000
1964/65	225,699	5,767	1993/94	20,000	21,000
1965/66	294,295	7,252	1994/95	137,787	26,000
1966/67	311,765	10,837	1995/96	340,000	39,500
1967/68	294,709	10,771	1996/97	542,000	36,500
1968/69	297,063	16,525	1997/98	560,000	49,000
1969/70	318,910	19,229	1998/99	547,000	50,000
1970/71	327,491	15,886	1999/00	675,000	53,000
1971/72	349,266	12,223	2000/01	0.902m	41,000
1972/73	439,785	16,018	2001/02	1.2m	43,104
1973/74	385,116	17,607	2002/03	1.48m	41,000
1974/75	385,416	17,209	2003/04	1.97m	42,000e
1975/76	367,514	12,323	2004/05	2.2m	43,000e

Sources: *The Aeroplane*, BAA and PIK.

Appendix Ten

Scottish Aviation Production

Pioneer 1	250hp DH Gipsy Queen 32/34. Span 52ft 9in. Gross, 4,126lb. two prototypes, converted to Pioneer 2.
Pioneer 2	520hp Alvis Leonides 501/4. Span 52ft 9in. Gross, 5,400lb. fifty-nine airframes completed. Delivered to the Royal Air Force, Royal Ceylon Air Force and Royal Malaysian Air Force and civilian operators.
Twin Pioneer	540hp Alvis Leonides 514. Span 76ft 6in. Gross, 14,200lb. Eighty-nine airframes completed. Delivered to the Royal Air Force, Royal Malaysian Air Force and civilian operators.
Bulldog	200hp Lycoming IO-360. Span 33ft. Gross, 2,350lb. 324 airframes completed, including one demonstrator and one civilian airframe. Delivered to the Royal Swedish Air Force, Royal Swedish Army, Royal Malaysian Air Force, Kenya Air Force, Royal Air Force, Ghana Air Force, Nigerian Air Force, Jordanian Royal Academy of Aeronautics, Royal Jordanian Air Force, Lebanese Defence Force, Kenya Air Force, Royal Hong Kong Auxiliary Air Force and the Botswana Air Defence Force.
Jetstream T.1	996shp Astazou XVID. Span 52ft. Gross, 12,500lb. Twenty-eight airframes completed for the Royal Air Force and Royal Navy. (See Appendix Eleven)
Jetstream 31/32	1020 shp Garrett TPE-331-12UAR. Span 52ft. Gross, 16,204 lb. 386 airframes completed for civilian operators and the Royal Navy.
Jetstream 41	1500 shp Garrett TFE-331-14. Span, 60ft. Gross, 22,377. 104 airframes completed for civilian operators.

Appendix Eleven

Military Astazou Jetstreams

This listing of twenty-eight military Astazou-powered Jetstreams shows the first two aircraft recovered from the United States. Eighteen airframes were from Jetstream Aircraft stock and Scottish Aviation built five new fuselages. The last two Jetstreams were acquired from civilian operators. All the military Jetstreams were converted to Mk.16 Astazou engines and became Series -200.

		First flown			
206	G-AWVJ	24.03.69	N1036S/SAL/XX475 RAF T.1/T.2 RN. From US	(1)	No.1
216	G-AXGL	16.0.69	N1037S/SAL/XX476 RAF T.1/T.2 RN. From US	(2)	No.2
249	G-AXXS	18.09.70	Terravia/SAL/XX477 RAF/T.1 RAF	Dbr 01.11.74	No.3
261	G-AXXT	14.10.73	Jetstream A/c/SAL/XX478 T.1 RAF/T.2 RN.	(3)	No.4
259	G-AXUR	27.10.73	Jetstream A/c/SAL/XX479 T.1 RAF/T.2 RN.	(4) Wfu	No.5
262	G-AXXU	13.02.74	Jetstream A/c/SAL/XX480 T.1 RAF/T.2 RN	(5) Wfu	No.6
251	G-AXUP	09.0374	Jetstream A/c/SAL/XX481 T.1 RAF/T.2 RN	(6)	No.7
263	nil	02.0474	Jetstream A/c/SAL/XX482 T.1 RAF/RN/RAF	(7) Wfu	No.8
264	nil	14.05.74	Jetstream A/c/SAL/XX483 T.1 RAF/T.2 RN	(8) Wfu	No.9
266	nil	31.05.74	Jetstream A/c/SAL/XX484 T.1 RAF/T.2 RN	(9)	No.10
268	nil	17.08.74	Jetstream A/c/SAL/XX485 T.1 RAF/T.2 RN	(10) *	No.11
265	nil	09.0874	Jetstream A/c/SAL/XX486 T.1 RAF/T.2 RN	(11)	No.12
269	nil	18.10.74	Jetstream A/c/SAL/XX487 T.1 RAF/T.2 RN	(12)	No.13
267	nil	2210.74	Jetstream A/c/SAL/XX488 T.1 RAF/T.2 RN	(13)	No.14
279	nil	31.10.75	Jetstream A/c/SAL/XX489 T.1 RAF	Cr. 8 May 1989	No.15
271	nil	17.11.75	Jetstream A/c/SAL/XX490 T.1 RAF/T.2 RN	(14) *	No.16
275	nil	12.11.75	Jetstream A/c/SAL/XX491 T.1 RAF	Cosford Museum	No.17
274	nil	06.11.74	Jetstream A/c/SAL/XX492 T.1 RAF	Newark Museum	No.18
278	nil	31.10.75	Jetstream A/c/SAL/XX493 T.1 RAF	Wfu	No.19
422	nil	T.116.10.75	SAL/XX494 T.1 RAF	Wfu	No.20
423	nil	T.101.10.75	SAL/XX495 T.1 RAF	Wfu	No.21
276	nil	31.10.75	Jetstream A/c/SAL/XX496 T.1 RAF	Cosford Museum	No.22
280	nil	25.03.76	Jetstream A/c/SAL/XX497 T.1 RAF	Wfu	No.23
424	nil	T.124.09.76	SAL/XX498 T.1 RAF	Wfu	No.24
425	nil	T.107.05.76	SAL/XX499 T.1 RAF	Wfu	No.25
426	nil	T.102.12.76	SAL/XX500 T.1 RAF	Wfu	No.2
248	GAXUO	23.02.70	F-BTMA/BAe/ZA110 T.2 RN	(15)	No.27
211	G-AXFV	24.04.69	9Q-CTC/BAe/ZA111 T.2 RN	(16)	No.28

* 268 and 271 were bought by the Uruguyan Navy in December 1998, as '875' and '876'.

References

PRO File, AIR.24/505-6, ATFERO ORB
PRO File, AIR.25/625-9, No.44 Group
PRO File, AIR.25/633, ditto
PRO File, AIR.25/639, ditto
PRO File, AIR.25/646-8, No.45 Group
PRO File, AIR.28/40, Ayr/Heathfield
PRO File, AIR.28/653-4, RAF Prestwick & TRP
PRO File, AIR.29/684, Grangemouth
PRO File, AIR.29/472, OAMCU, ORB
PRO File, AIR.29/473, TAC, ORB
PRO File, AIR.29/598, Prestwick
PRO File, AIR.28/23, Monthly Receipts & Deliveries, 1940–45
PRO File, AIR.38/26 & 64, No.45 Group
PRO File, AIR.38/199 & 227, 44 Group History.
National Defence HQ, Ottowa File, DHH79/1 L.

Atlantic Bridge, HMSO, 1945
'Report on the Progress of Civil Aviation 1939-1945', HMSO, 1946
'Prestwick Air Letter, 1950-2004', David Reid and James Riach
The Army Air Forces in WW2, Craven & Cate, 1958
I'll Take the High Road, Sholto Watt, 1960
Aviation in Scotland, Gillies & Wood, 1966
The Forgotten Pilots, Lettice Curtis, 1971
Prestwick 1975, Noel Capper, Royal Aeronautical Society, 1975
Ferry Command, Don McVicar, 1981
Ferryman, Air Cdr. Powell, 1982
Golden Jubilee, Jim Ewart, Scottish Airports, 1985
Master Airman, (D.C.T. Bennett), Alan Bramson, 1985
Lion Rampant & Winged, Robertson, 1986
Scotland Scanned, Wiggins & Reid, 1986
Thirty West, Peter Berry, 1996
Lend-Lease Aircraft in World War II, Arthur Pearcy, 1996
RAF Flying Training & Support Units, Air-Britain, 1997
Airfield Research Group Review, Barry Abraham
Trans-Atlantic Air Deliveries, 1940-46, Peter Berry, 1998
'Airfield Focus', No.42, Prestwick Airport, GMS Enterprises, Peter Berry, 2000

United States Air Force in Britain, 2000, Robert Jackson
Tail Ends of the Fifties, Peter Campbell
Just One of the Pioneers, Bookcraft, William T. Neil, 2002
Turbo Prop Airliner Production List, Eastwood & Roach, 2003
Air Arsenal North America, Midland Counties, Butler & Hagedorn, 2004
Prestwick's Pioneer, A Portrait of David F. McIntyre, Dougal McIntyre, 2004

Index